What

Nina Impala

Dearly Departed: What I Learned About Living from the Dying

Dedication

I dedicate this book to my mom, Antoinette
Impala.

My heart starts here . . .

*For what is it to die but to stand naked in the wind
and to melt into the sun?*

*And what is it to cease breathing, but to free the
breath
from its restless tides, that it may rise and expand
and seek God unencumbered?*

*Only when you drink from the river of silence shall
you
indeed sing.*

*And when you reached the mountain top. then you
shall
begin to climb.*

*And when the earth shall claim your limbs then
shall
you truly dance.*

Kahlil Gibran

Contents

Introduction

In 1997 I made an impulsive and spontaneous
decision to go to massage school. I thought I was
being spontaneous but I have the feeling the
universe was putting things in place to help me
find my natural healing ability. In retrospect, I
realize my healing gift had always been there; I
just hadn't known it was part of me until one day,
in the middle of a massage session my client
suddenly blurted out, "Did you know you have so
much heat coming from your hands?"

The truth was I didn't know. I was very new
to massage at this stage and this comment from a
complete stranger felt like some kind of sign that I
needed to pay attention to. It led me to learn about
Therapeutic Touch and Reiki Healing. My gift
through touch is what I have been called to do for
some time now. There is so much power in touch,
and even the lightest lingering touch relaxes
people and makes them feel loved. Once I
understood the power of touch I knew I had found
my calling and it has become my passionate
vocation.

My purpose in writing this book is to take
you into a time and experience we will all have
someday. It is my hope that you will have a shift in
thinking about death and dying and hopefully

come to see the beauty in the process. Through the stories in this book I want to show you that death doesn't have to be a scary end, but instead can be a new beginning that brings great lightness of being. My experiences as a hospice volunteer and the lessons I learned from the dying have had a life changing affect on me even to this day.

A hospice volunteer is a non-clinical person that comes into a home or facility and simply becomes a friend to the dying—a friend that gives time, attention and support without expecting anything in return. Although the gifts of working with the dying are non-tangible they are gifts of the heart that remain with us long after our patients are gone. All hospice workers are special people, but the hospice volunteers that start with little or no experience are truly precious. Simply put, they are people that know there is a need, and want to help, or maybe they had a hospice experience within their own family that tugged at their hearts to answer the call. Hospice work is not for everyone, which is something I hear nearly every day.

There is another side to death that people like me, who approach dying in a different way, are privileged to see. I do not deny that death can seem scary, sad, and painful to watch. But the fact is that death is as natural as birth. It's a transition, a rebirth, a journey into the next life.

What I want to share with you through this book is that there are many ways of experiencing

death, as a person with a terminal illness, or as a
friend or family member of a terminally ill person.
And I want to do this by sharing the wisdom and
love imparted to me through my experiences as a
hospice volunteer. The truth is that just like birth,
death is a sacred event. We are ALL holy and when
we pass we are simply returning to where we
came from. It is a sacred event that we ALL will
experience someday. My hope is that after reading
this book you will not only find peace about death;
but that you also will be inspired to share this with
others, or possibly even consider becoming a
hospice volunteer yourself.

Most of the stories you will read are from my
own experiences with patient care volunteering,
and I have changed the names of patients, family
members and others to protect their privacy.
Being with the dying and their loved ones is a
powerful experience, and teaching others about
the profound journey we take just this one time in
our life truly is a life-altering experience for all
involved. I know it has always had a profound
effect on me.

The one question I am most often asked by
other volunteers is why do I feel happy when I
leave a dying person? The answer I give is that
when you're with someone who is making his or
her transition everything you thought was so
important in your life seems to disappear. When
you are standing at the bedside, holding a hand, or

just being present with the dying, guess who is right next-door? The angels and loved ones who have already crossed over are blessing us, thanking us for assisting their loved ones home. Angels, relatives and other loved ones that have passed on, are all so very glad when someone is there with the dying to bring comfort and support as they make their transition. What a holy gift to bring to another human being! The realization of the sacredness of the journey into death often gives me goose bumps, particularly when I leave the bedside of a patient who is very close to their time.

Our time here is short. It really is. Hospice volunteer work has taught me this as well as many powerful things about letting go. Each and every patient has gifted me with valuable insights that will never leave my heart. To learn to see with your heart is quite an experience.

Let me explain what it means to see with your heart. Imagine yourself walking for the first time into the room of someone who is in the final stages of cancer. Your first impression may be how the person looks physically. Maybe they are very thin, or full of fluid, or their breathing is labored, the sound of an oxygen machine fills the room, and sad family members sit close by. That's one way to walk in the room. There is another far more effective and compassionate way.

Before I enter, I always take a deep breath and carry an inner smile in my heart to provide

unseen strength and support to assist the person
who will be passing soon. My heart becomes my
"eyes" and instead of seeing all the sadness, pain,
and angst, I see something much greater taking
place: I see a beautiful transition in progress. With
my "heart-sight" I bring my energy of inner
knowing and peace to the patient, not sorrow or
worry. Sorrow and worry carry heaviness into the
room. My goal is to bring light to the individual for
his or her transition, and HeartSight™ does this.
When I just rely on my regular eyesight I see all
the sadness and negatives and my mind will
become too involved at a time when I really need
to detach from that and work from my heart. As a
hospice worker I consider this to be my job. But
I'm not the only one who can bring in this
HeartSight™. Family members and loved ones can
bring a completely different feeling to the dying by
seeing with their own hearts as well.

My highest hope in writing this book and
sharing the stories of my journey with hospice
patients is that you will find it easier to respond
from your heart to help those you love make their
transition, and to release any fears you may have
regarding your own mortality and your own
future.

Chapter 1

My Mom

You're in my eyes.
How else could I see light?

You're in my brain
This wild Joy
If love did not live in matter
How would any place have
Any hold on anyone -Rumi

As I was in the process of writing this book my mom, who was 75 at the time, was in the end stage of cancer, and I was on the biggest hospice journey of my life. As is my practice with all my patients, I stayed present while stepping aside and allowing her to do whatever she needed to do to prepare herself for the most sacred event of her life—her transition into the next.

Mom was diagnosed with breast cancer at 72, just after a trip to Sicily. When she was first hospitalized we were told she had maybe three days to live. There was no way my mother was going to accept that diagnosis. She wanted to live, and her prayer was, "I want more time with my kids." And that is what she did for the next three years. Then the cancer became more aggressive. Fluids needed to be extracted from her body often, and chemotherapy had to be started again owing to fluid retention. My sister would say, "Her cancer weeps." I will never forget that: a cancer that weeps. I often wonder, was it weeping for mom as it slowly took her life? Was it weeping the tears that she had never shed? Or was it weeping for a life cut short?

My mom was strong, a fighter, a dreamer, fiercely independent, funny, creative and beautiful. She had been both a wonderful mother and a good friend, especially when I was grown and we would talk about everything. Mom always "knew" things, in just the same way that I always know, when one of my sons call, if there is something bothering them. I can just feel it. It is what we moms do. If I was having a challenging day and I called Mom to say hi, she would always know; she could somehow hear it in my voice, even when I tried to hide it.

I miss that.

I know I was not the easiest child to raise. I was the challenging kid, the one that did things differently, and stirred things up. When I was young I was also sick. I had to be medicated for about eight years for hives, which is not an uncommon symptom in people who are energetically sensitive (though I didn't figure this out until I was much older). The hives got really ugly, even disfiguring. I could not go out in public because my face, hands and feet would swell up so severely it would be hard to walk, see or even talk. But Mom always found a way to make it okay, and I depended on her for comfort as children do with their mothers. I can only imagine how much she worried about this little girl with the strange hives.

She was involved in everything when we were growing up. We always had extra people at our house for dinner parties and the like, and as we were raised devout Catholics, priests and nuns were regular guests. It always felt quite special to have a nun or a priest sitting at the table; they smelled good to me. I can still recall that smell, and it was so comforting to get hugs from them.

Mom was intricately involved with the Catholic Church, which was a big part of our lives. I look back on this today and realize that my Catholic upbringing was one of the biggest gifts my mom gave to me; it set the foundation at a very young age for me to become the person I am now.

We prayed the rosary as a family, celebrated feast days, and even went on a ski vacation with Father Kennedy, a priest friend who had a heavy Irish accent and a great sense of humor. And we frequently went on pilgrimages. Of course our pilgrimages weren't to exotic places in Europe or on other continents. Our pilgrimages were closer to home. For example, we sometimes drove to Burbank, California and hiked up a dirt hill with all my cousins to bring a flower crown to place atop a

statue of The Blessed Mother. At our church, St.
Elizabeth's in Pasadena, California, we had a
beautiful grotto that was reminiscent of "Madonna
at the Rocks" by Da Vinci, though not the Madonna
part, just the rock part. To a young girl it felt like a
special place to pray where things happened, and I
used to kneel in front of it, knowing deep in my
heart that by praying in that spot a miracle would
happen. There were also sacred times that we
celebrated. May was a special month in our home
because it was Mary's month. It was a busy time in
our household and my wonderful Sicilian
grandmother, who always kept Mary close by,
celebrated this time of the Virgin Mother carefully
placing statues, pictures and altars in her house,
which is something I still do today. Our faith was
not just a Sunday thing; we lived it.

Mom also loved investigating the apparitions
that were seen in different parts of the world. She
knew so much about Lourdes and Medjugorje, and
she had a book about the four girls in Garabandal,
Spain to whom the Blessed Mother appeared to
reveal a great miracle to come as a warning to
mankind. This story was all over the news and was
very controversial in 1967. As a young girl I was
captivated by the story and wanted to know more.
I read the book and saw the pictures of the girls in
states of spiritual ecstasy; their feet barely
touching the ground, faces tilted upward with a

light emanating from them. The energy of this
event has stayed with me for years.

All the experiences that were part of my
religious upbringing, and the miraculous
apparitions by the girls at Garabandal, had a huge
impact on me. At the time I didn't realize they
would be so important in leading me to my
vocation of helping others. Much of what I do
today comes from the faith that my mother
brought into my life as a young girl. I would have
to say that my Catholicism also contributed largely
to the vocation I have with helping the dying.
Mother Mary will always be constant in my life,
and my prayers to Her have always brought me
peace and restored my faith. Today, in order to
help all people, I am now open to all faiths, and my
belief is that there is no right or wrong way to
know God.

Mom watched my own spiritual process
unfold as I grew and started massage school,
began the practice of Reiki healing, and began
moving deeper and deeper into the spiritual life.
When I started doing Reiki, Mom was open to it,
but she also knew I was going into new areas with
my faith, that it was a big step for me, and that not
everyone would be comfortable with it. She
warned me that some people would not accept
what I was doing, but I did not care. I told her
many times, "Mom we are not that different. I am a
little rebel just like you, searching for the meaning

of this life through faith," to which she would simply smile at me and nod her head.

I don't know if she would agree, but sometimes I think Mom and I were very alike in the way we lived our lives. When Mom left Dad after 35 years of marriage it was to reconnect with who she, Antoinette, was. She took so much flack from the extended family for her choices, but she trudged on and learned a lot about herself. She didn't care what others thought. She just did what she felt she needed to do. I got that independent spirit from her, and I am proud of it. While she was still alive, and I was going through a big life change, Mom said to me, "Nina, you have always followed your heart, and it has not steered you wrong." I loved hearing that from her, as it confirmed my decision at the time and helped me to know that I was doing the right thing for me.

My mother opened my heart with her love for God. She was the strong sturdy ship that weathered many of life's storms, including storms with a sick but spirited child like me. According to Mom, I was special from the start. "You were my baby born breech and face up!" She said. "I knew you were special then."

And so was she.

As mom's disease progressed I would drive ninety minutes each way every week to be with her, to love and take care of her, and to give her Reiki when she allowed it. The best part about this story of how I came to be what I am today, is that I had the opportunity to tell her how much her love and teaching meant to me. I was able to share with her how, as a young sick girl, my Catholic faith has brought me so much consolation. It felt wonderful to tell her how fortunate I felt to have had so many comforting holy things in my life. When she replied, "Oh Nina, that makes me feel all warm inside," I felt such a sense of completion.

Chapter 2

Magical Mary Ann

*As essence turns to ocean
The particles glisten.*

*Watch how in this candle flame instant
Blaze all the moments you have lived -Rumi*

People are always asking me, "How can you do that?"

"What," I say, "be with a dying person?"

Their faces scrunch and they look sad and shake their heads and say, "I could never do that."

Most people like to take death and tuck it away in a very dark place and pretend its not going to come. I try to educate them about the beauty in death. Regardless of whether the person dying experiences a good transition or a non-peaceful one, there is always a higher knowledge or unseen forces at work. There are no accidents. You're reading this book because you attracted this experience, and that's a good thing.

My favorite reply to people who inquire about how I can be with the dying is my standard and most beautiful divine answer, "I love it because I get to work on Sacred Ground and I can feel my wings."

My very first patient, Mary Ann, gifted me with these attributes. Mary Ann had cancer. She was living with her daughter, husband and grandchildren in a delightful home out in the country. As I took the scenic drive out to her family home there were horses, expansive houses, and wide-open skies. I was excited but had no idea what to expect as I walked up to the front door, introduced myself to the family, and was led upstairs to meet Mary Ann.

She was laying in a king size bed. It was so large I needed a step stool to reach her. As I approached she opened her arms wide and asked, "Why are you here? What can you bring me?"

I answered with the question, "I am a Reiki practitioner?"

Mary Ann's face lit up! "That's wonderful," she squealed.

I had no idea she even knew what this was, and back in the late 90's Reiki healing was not as popular as it is now. Actually Reiki was considered to be "out there," and in fact, *way* out there for some. Simply stated, Reiki is a peaceful energetic hands-on healing technique that I was specially trained in, and use to this day. You will hear me refer to it frequently, and if you want more details, www.reiki.org is an excellent website to visit. Even if we don't know or practice a healing modality we *all* have healing energy that comes through us. It is part of loving. Think about the last time someone you cared about was sad and you wanted to touch or hug him or her. It is a natural response to comfort and give love. Love brings healing.

While doing hospice work it has become evident to me from the responses of my patients, that healing comes through touch, whether I'm aware of it or not. I believe the simple act of touching has a very therapeutic effect. Touch is very healing regardless of whether or not it is Reiki healing. As it turned out Mary Ann loved receiving Reiki and I gave her Reiki healing every time I was there.

Mary Ann was extremely metaphysical. She had moved around a lot in her life, and had tried everything. I loved listening to her talk about her experiences. I was intrigued, as I was just starting to open up to the world of metaphysics, and although I was brought up Catholic my heart was searching for more truth. Mary Ann had the wisdom of this truth. The books that surrounded her in her room were testament to many years spent researching different healing modalities and connections to the spirit world.

One day when I was with Mary Ann she showed me pictures of a house she had lived in back in the 70's. She had erected a large pyramid in the back yard. It was open and made out of some kind of metal. It was fascinating to me, and, as always, she would light up when she talked about it. She studied all faiths, and her shelves where filled with poetry and prayers from everywhere in the world.

After I had been visiting Mary Ann for a couple of months her legs became very swollen, confining her to the upper floor. She felt so isolated from the family that they decided to bring her downstairs to give her a little bit more space. Mary Ann was happy with that as they made sure she had all her little treasures around her. I would sit with her and listen to her tell stories about each little treasure and what it meant to her. Mary Ann loved dolphins and did quite a bit of work with them. I remember her telling me she talked with dolphins! I thought, *Wow, I want to do that.* She laughed a lot and was certainly playful like the dolphins. She also shared her wisdom about the healing energies of crystals and the power that pyramids hold. She showed me pictures and loaned me books;, I felt so honored to have such a wonderful woman as my patient.

As Mary Ann approaches the last days of her life here, something very special happened, involving a beautiful picture that someone had painted for her, and that her family had hung where should could see and enjoy it.

Caring for the dying can be very tiring and emotional, and we were all pretty exhausted in the last days of Mary Ann's life. Her daughter, Connie, was amazing and cared for Mary Ann with love and gentleness; the love between mother and daughter was beautiful to watch. During this time something astonishing happened to Mary Ann's painting, which depicted rainbows shining on rolling hills, and fields with green and golden hues.

One day I noticed that the rays of light depicted in the painting had become brighter and larger. I said to Connie "Did that picture change or am I just tired?"

She looked right at me and said, "I was wondering about that, because I thought I was going crazy. It *has* changed. The light beaming down *is* a lot brighter and larger!" We both knew that the light in the painting was a reflection of Mary Ann's dying process.

Mary Ann had huge faith in all of life. She was a true believer in heaven, angels, and divine beings of all kinds, and so she knew that she was never ever alone. As her time grew closer her daughter wanted her to die peacefully and easily, as we all would wish for anyone coming to the end of life. However Mary Ann lingered for a very long time. What I learned from witnessing a body lingering even though it is barely here, is that the soul does not leave until it's ready. When a family member lingers it is one of the most difficult things on earth for us to witness. This is not a peaceful time for the caregiver, especially when they feel their loved one is suffering. I have been asked questions like, "Why has she not died yet? Why is she still here?

How can she still be alive? It's not fair, why would God have her suffer like this!"

In spite of being emotionally and physically exhausted, caregivers and family members and friends often experience feelings of guilt about wanting their loved one to die. Plus, sometimes, as was the case with Mary Ann, there are small children and other family members living in the home who also require care and attention. End of life care can take its toll on everyone involved.

Mary Ann's lingering death affected me as well, and at the time it was very hard for me to wrap my head around the *why's* of this kind of crossing. Let me share with you what brings me peace in these types of situations now.

With any loss in life our human side is always looking for the means to an end. In the time between the beginning of the person's journey of death and the time they make their transition, the soul is still evolving and completing its process. These periods of discomfort and growth occur throughout life and are a vital part of the dying process. Some people lay still for days and some experience "terminal agitation" or restlessness, which usually occurs when death is near. It is very important to assess the patient's physical condition to see if there is anything that may be causing the patient distress, and then do everything possible to make them comfortable. Calm, soothing music can be played and candles lit in the room. Care should be taken to ensure the temperature in the room remains comfortable.

Family members may feel uncomfortable, both for the individual making the transition, as well as for others in the room around them. Being uncomfortable in any situation, especially a tough one, usually means that you are learning something important. Being with the dying has taught me that even as someone prepares to leave this world there may still be some learning for them, or someone close to them, to do before they actually make their transition.

I did not know this at the time of Mary Ann's passing, but over the years, through my experiences with the dying, I have noticed that often people die the way they have lived. Mary Ann led a very free-spirited mystical life, searching out and learning everything she could about the magical world around her, and she continued seeking this knowledge until her very last breath. She was determined to *experience* her dying process and not be "out of it," so she refused to use any morphine. What courage she had! Throughout her life, Mary Ann had embraced and gleaned all that she could from the trials and tribulations that came with being human, and this is how she died. This Indian Prayer was on Mary Ann's memorial card:

Spirit I am, One with the Creator

Free of All Limits
Safe, Healed and Whole.

I became very close to Mary Ann; I prayed by her bedside, and I strongly sensed her desire to leave her body. The night she died, I felt her go. In fact, I felt her so much I nearly left with her. I remember getting up and thinking, *I need to take a shower and get back into my body!* It felt like my feet were not touching the ground. My body was walking to the shower but my spirit was trying to go with Mary Ann. At that time in my life, I remember feeling very alone like I was delving into some area that was forbidden. The only person I knew to ask about my experience with Mary Ann was the Jesuit priest at the Catholic chapel up the hill from me, but his words had little impact on me. I did realize that my ability to access the other side so easily was a gift and that I needed to learn how to use it in a more grounded and positive way. My experience with Mary Ann taught me so much about the path I was embarking on, and through my experiences I came to realize that God was preparing me to be with the dying for many years to come. I thank God and Mary Ann to this day for setting me on the beautiful and loving path of hospice volunteering.

Chapter 3

Estelle, the Desert, and Ice Cream

*"Each of us is here to discover our true selves; that
essentially we are spiritual beings who have taken
manifestation in physical form; that we're not
human beings that have occasional spiritual
experiences, that we're spiritual beings that have
occasional human experiences."*
—*Deepak Chopra*

At 87, Estelle had the warmest eyes I've ever seen.
When I reflect on my time with her, and recall her
smile, my heart lights up and my face glows. My
visits with Estelle were filled with wonderful deep
conversations about life as we ate watermelon, her
favorite, and her kitty roamed about.

As with Mary Ann, when I first met Estelle
she seemed to have been expecting me. Her first
words were, "Are you ready for this?" Then she
looked directly into my eyes, and said, " I am so
glad we could be together again. I have been
waiting for you!"

Those words shot through me like cupid's
arrow, and as I gazed into her eyes, I instantly had
that feeling that we *had* been together before.

There is something to be said about direct
"lingering" eye contact. It is a silent recognition
that goes right through to the soul, and Estelle and
I saw into each other's. From that moment on
Estelle and I were going on her dying journey hand
in hand. But I promised myself no matter what
happened, my feet needed to stay firmly planted
on the ground this time! (A note to prospective
volunteers: healthy boundaries are necessary!)

When I arrived at Estelle's house, it had just
been flooded, and she was trying to dry everything
out. Apparently, this was not an unusual incident,
and this scenario happened a couple more times
while she was still in her little apartment. Estelle
had the sweetest little apartment that backed up
to luscious rolling hills in the Temecula Valley. The
wind always blew every afternoon bringing with it
a hint of beach air. Bunnies would come visit just
outside her patio, and the view from this tiny little
apartment was Estelle's little miracle, overlooking
lush green, peaceful hills that rolled right up to her
front door. The apartment was situated at the back
of a low-income housing complex for seniors. It
was perfect for Estelle, and she enjoyed her
freedom and independence.

As the stories started to flow I realized that
Estelle was very open in her thinking and quite
mystical, so I soon became hungry for every
morsel that came out of her mouth. Just like Mary
Ann, Estelle had chosen a spiritual path in her
lifetime. She was exceptionally intuitive, and had

ventured into many spiritual arenas that most
would not have gone to in her day. It took great
courage to do this in her time.

I regularly gave Estelle massage as well as
many Reiki treatments. She was truly grateful and
she taught me much about my own intuitive
abilities. She was 100% correct about a guy I was
dating at the time. I remember her looking straight
at me with her sparkly baby blues and saying,
"Nina that guy is no good for you." And boy was
she right!

Estelle would make me laugh as we talked
about different faiths. She would say, "You know
Nina, my neighbors think that I am going to hell
because I am not a Christian woman," And I would
lovingly nudge her shoulder and say, "You're not
going to hell, Estelle. They just don't know you."

I reminded her that we both knew there is no
right or wrong way to be with God, that as long as
you know Him, that's all that matters. I wish, I pray
that people would realize this: Love always wins,
God is Love, and God comes to us in countless
ways! Estelle knew this; she had a heart full of
wisdom. She also knew that if she had said
anything to her neighbors they would have
thought she was loony. Since we didn't want to
add any more judgment to the situation we simply
decided that the best way to deal with this was to
bless the neighbors on their own journey

One of my most beautiful experiences with Estelle was when she asked me to drive her to Palm Springs to see a friend. We'd had many conversations about her friend, and she had written him and received no reply. She was worried and needed to see him. I sensed it was very important to her that she connect with him before she died. I'll admit I was a little nervous and I felt like I was kidnapping her by not telling anyone that we were going. In my heart I knew it was the right thing to do. Her cancer protruded from her chest, and was about the size of a racquetball. Every time I would see it I would be reminded of how fragile Estelle was and that her time was ticking away.

So, off we went to see her friend. I carefully put Estelle in my car; adjusting her seat up, down, backwards and forwards to make sure she was comfortable on our little field trip. I grabbed some water bottles and off we went. She was such a little trooper. Estelle had lived in the desert for many years and had not been out there for a long time. Many memories surfaced for her and I listened to the extraordinary stories of the life this courageous woman had lived, taking risks for what she believed in.

It was extremely hot in the desert on this day, around 110 degrees or so. Her friend lived in a skilled nursing facility. When we arrived I found a shady spot to park, helped Estelle from the car, and let her lead the way as we walked. The place was typical of a skilled nursing facility, with a large front desk, nurses and health aides bustling about, seniors in wheel chairs everywhere, and an occasional cry or moan in the background. Sadly, facilities like this are the last stop for many. I was glad that Estelle was going to have the opportunity to see her friend, now.

We waited at the front desk, and the staff seemed inquisitive about these old friends who were reuniting. I could feel Estelle's anticipation for their meeting. When they first laid eyes on each other my heart melted and I knew they had been more than just friends. He was dying too. My heart could barely take in what I was experiencing; two dying people saying goodbye. He was in a wheel chair and very weak. As I stood there watching, Estelle looked at me with her big baby blues and said, "Can you find us some ice cream?"

The senior assisted living facility was in a remote spot. I remember driving to it thinking, *where is this place?* There were no markets, pharmacies, or even other houses, but there *was* a hospital nearby. Even in the 110-degree heat I was determined to get cold ice cream so this beautiful couple could share their last dessert together. The magnitude of this blew me away. I wanted un-melted ice cream! Thankfully, the hospital was only about two blocks away, but I drove there thinking it would be faster and the ice cream would not melt.

Why is it that hospital cafeterias always seem to be tucked away in some distant corner of the building at the end of a maze of hallways? When I finally found it, I discovered they had soft serve ice cream that comes out of a machine. It was perfect! When I explained to the cashier what I was doing she double wrapped the containers, and off I went. I felt like the rabbit in Alice in Wonderland, scurrying through the maze of the hospital saying, *"I'm late, I'm late for a very important date. No time to say hello goodbye, I'm late, I'm late I'm late!"*

Success! I arrived and presented Estelle and her friend with their delicious un-melted ice cream. Then I left them alone and sat in my car and waited for sweet Estelle to come out when she was ready. I could not believe the stamina Estelle had in spite of the cancerous tumor growing out of her body.

Not long after our field trip Estelle starting showing signs of noticeable decline. On one of my visits she had overdosed on some of her medication. Her eyes were huge and glassy looking, and her house had just flooded again. She offered me watermelon the moment I walked in, and I knew something was terribly wrong. She sat on the couch, pink watermelon juice dripping from her mouth, talking a mile a minute, though some of her words were slurred. Tearing up a bit, as I do from time to time with my patients, I called my hospice agency and let them know she might not be able to live safely by her self any more. It was a turning point for all involved, including her daughter, who ended up taking Estelle home with her.

Many times when a loved one is dying at home with the family, healings take place on many levels for everyone involved. As I mentioned earlier, unfinished business can be a little uncomfortable and push one to the edge of comfort, but oh, the gift that comes from the loss. Mother Teresa was a woman who gifted the world with her wisdom as well as her compassion for those experiencing great loss. Her long time friend, Eileen Eagan, after complaining about the world's problems, was asked by Mother Teresa if there were another word she could use instead of the word problems. When Eileen could not think of one that carried the same weight, Mother Teresa simply said, "Why not use the word gift?"

Life's challenges and loss can seem insurmountable when taking care of a terminally ill family member. Challenges show up in many forms. One of the biggest challenges I frequently witness is that the caregiver often becomes consumed by the care giving. As the caregiver's life comes to a halt and everything becomes about the patient, exhaustion and anxiety take a toll and resentments can build. If a relationship was not that good to begin with, caring for a dying loved one can be very challenging, The good thing is I almost always get to witness the miracles of healing between family members before the patient passes. There are no accidents in this process. Whenever we are going through the challenges of loss, all we usually think of is how we can make it stop or make it end. Remember, the soul is trying to evolve and will take the time it needs to do so. There is no rushing through the process. The important thing to focus on is the time we have with the person who is dying. Our mind can keep us in a prison of suffering if the crisis of loss is all we focus on.

Give yourself some time when you're in the thick of these challenging times. Don't try to hurry yourself past the pain and panic of what has occurred. Open your heart, take a breath, sit down for a bit, and stop. Stop the streaming thoughts of how and why this has happened and what comes next. Take a few really slow deep breaths to quiet your very busy mind, and tell yourself that you can do this. *You can do it!* Just Breathe. Breathe in Peace. Breathe in, *I am okay.* Breathe in, *I am not alone.* Say out loud so you can hear yourself, "I am not alone."

That's faith and trust.

Once you find that bit of peace within, where you are focused only on the here and now, this present moment, notice how it feels to just sit in this space and *be.* Listen to your heart, not your head. You know the voice. It's the voice of spirit, the one that does not judge you, or tell you, "Hey! Get going! What are you doing just sitting here?"

No, it's a quiet voice that says, "I have missed you, and I am here to help you. You don't have to do this alone, but you need to stop and listen. You can't hear me over all that fearful noise in your head."

Being in the present is vital for a better life in general and for getting through the transition process of a loved one. Living too much in the past or in the future can be especially dangerous during loss. It can keep you in a state of fear and stop you from enjoying the time you have left.

When you can become mindful of being in the present moment, fear will be replaced by love and the endless gifts of the spirit will help you through whatever it is you are experiencing.

Think of being in the present moment like a meditation because it is a practice of sorts and learning to make it second nature will truly be a gift to you. The breath is very helpful in doing this, so is a walk out in nature even if it is just a couple of minutes. Have you heard the quote by Eleanor Roosevelt? "Yesterday is history, tomorrow is a mystery, but today is a gift. That's why they call it present." It's the truth!

After a loved one dies it is so important for the living as well as the deceased to have found peace around a relationship or situation. Estelle's transition process was an inspiring example of this.

Beautiful Estelle and her wonderful daughter had unfinished business. Neither had expressed their feelings in the past so their communication was strained. Old resentments hung around them like dark clouds. I knew they loved each other, and I also knew that they had old wounds that needed to heal before Estelle left. Over the last week of Estelle's life, miracles of healing took place and years of suffering and emotional pain on both sides were healed. What I learned from my time with Estelle and her daughter helped me later on with my Dad's passing.

God gives us these beautiful opportunities to heal broken relationships and clear old hurts and fears before we, or someone we love, move on. If our hearts are open to the experience and we do not allow our fear to block the healing, the gifts for everyone are just waiting to be opened. The soul feels the joy and gratitude.

I believe if business is left unfinished it doesn't just go away, it shows up in every area of one's life, and I also believe that if the deceased have left with unfinished business they still suffer. I know they are assisted with this and are loved on the other side, but unfinished issues from this life still need to be worked through. Estelle and her family taught us that it's much better to let the love flow and flow. And as I stated earlier, whether you are the one departing or the one saying goodbye, you are never alone in this process. The angels love to assist us, and they are always

present with the dying. All you have to do is ask
them to be with you too.

As a side note, the quote from Mother Teresa
came to me as a gift within a greeting card in the
grocery store one day, at a time when the world
was heavy for me. I have never seen a quote from
Mother Teresa in a card at the grocery store since.

Chapter 4

Terri, Never Forgotten

*"I am not sure exactly what heaven will be like, but I
know that when we die and it comes time for God to
judge us, he will not ask, 'How many good things
have you done in your life?' rather he will ask, 'How
much love did you put into what you did?"* —Mother
Teresa

Terri was 44 and I was 38 when I became her
hospice care volunteer. When I made my first visit
to Terri's tiny house I found her in a bed in the
living room. Terri was quiet, and I got the feeling
she just needed someone to be like a girlfriend.
She was curious about me and also about what a
hospice volunteer did, so I explained to her that I
would be coming over just to spend time with
her—nothing medical. I let her know I was there
for support in whatever way she needed. I could
go to the grocery store, do the dishes for her, or we
could just sit and chat. I was there to listen. Our
relationship quickly blossomed into friendship,
and we really were girlfriends in the end. Normally
hospice volunteers are the givers, not expecting
anything in return. Even though hospice staff
understand this, and we give of ourselves freely,

our giving always comes back to us in ways we could never imagine. Such was the case with my relationship with Terri.

The journey with Terri was very different than what I had experienced with other patients. The household had four generations living in it, and, owing to a rough past, was less than stable. With Terri's imminent death approaching the family was barely functioning. Though Terri was surrounded by family members, and they were all having a difficult time dealing with her illness in one way or another—except for her son Jaden with whom she shared the same birthday. Jaden was sixteen when I started visiting his mom, and he was her rock. His mother's death would change his life forever, but he didn't let that keep him from being a supportive and loving angel. Jaden possessed a certain wisdom that Terri recognized. She drew strength from it, and her love for him kept her alive for that year.

Terri's husband was not around much though he visited a couple of times. He was dealing with his own troubled past. Her daughter, Suzie had two babies, one of which was born during the year I was there. Suzie was in a tumultuous relationship and using drugs. It was very hard to watch, because the babies were not being cared for properly. Terri's mother rarely came out of her room when I was there, and when she did, she always seemed disturbed and upset.

Stuck at the dead center of household activity, Terri had no private sanctuary to call her own, and she and I never really had time alone. Sometimes Suzie would storm in yelling and screaming, occasionally even at me! If the weather was nice Terri and I would sit outside. Terri smoked, but I didn't care. After all, she was dying, and it was all she had to call her own. In spite of the lack of privacy we had long talks about Terri's past, and I allowed her to unload the huge baggage of regret and resentments whenever she needed to. We talked about God, and her fear of death. As her time grew closer, she wanted to learn more about my spiritual world, and I gave her Reiki.

One day we had an amazing conversation, which confirmed for me that the angels are constantly working through me. Terri and I were talking about the actual moment of death and what happens. I wanted to comfort her, and so , knowing this was something we had both experienced, I explained to that death was like a birth,. I said to her, "You know when we are pregnant the baby is in our tummy growing and changing inside of us as it is preparing for its birth. When it's time to be born there are signs for the mom that the baby is coming. At the time of birth many people will be there, waiting for the arrival of this child. I believe dying is very much like this; it will be peaceful and before you know it you will be looking into the faces of those you love. With open arms they will be welcoming you, saying 'C'mon Terri, its beautiful here. We love you.'"

When I went home and told my mom this story, mom's eyes grew big with amazement, and she said, "I have a letter for you."

My "Auntie" Eleanor had lived with my mother when she was growing up, and she was considered a sister. She had become a nun and was diagnosed with cancer at a very young age. The year on the letter mom gave me was 1967—I was just seven years old at that time. My mom was so sad that she was going to lose her sister. Auntie Eleanor had written mom a letter about what was taking place and told her not to be sad. It read:

> Supposing a child in his mother's womb at the ninth-month period would argue that he did not want to be born. It is so nice and warm and safe in the darkness of the mother's womb. He gets all the nourishment he needs, and after all, what does he know about the world out there? And supposing his mother could answer all his objections: 'Come on out and be born! It's beautiful on this side. You'll be safe because I love you. Come on out and be born. Come look into the face of the one who loves you!"

Auntie Eleanor had been working through me to help Terri, and I knew it with all my heart.

There were times at Terri's that were hard, especially with the drug issues, Suzie, and the babies; many times it was probably not that safe for me. But Terri needed me. She did not have any girlfriends, and I knew how much she appreciated my presence in her life. At one point the Hospice coordinator told me that if I needed to stop I could, but I could never do that; I'd been with Terry almost a year and I was committed to stay with her to the end.

In 1998 I still prayed the Rosary and it will always be a sacred part of me. Italian Catholics always pray the Rosary; we prayed it as a family, and miracles always came from it. I would pray the Rosary to prepare myself while on the drive to Terri's house. As I would get out of the car, step on to the curb, and walk towards the house, I would do it mindfully. When I would leave and step off of the curb I literally felt as if I was stepping back into another world, and usually prayed the Rosary on the way back home.

One of the main lessons I learned with Terri and her family was how important it is to remain neutral. There were a lot of issues in Terri's family, and I had to put aside judgment. But I also needed to be smart and take care of myself, so I could continue to see Terri. It was not my job to fix any of the other family members; my job was to be there for Terri.

Terri barely had enough money to live on let alone take care of everyone else's needs, and she ended up having to move shortly before her death. I thought it was so unfair. She had become so weak; Hospice and I helped her out the best we could. Her bed was again placed in the living room of a tiny little two-bedroom apartment, where she would live with Suzie and the babies.

At Christmas time, which was close to the time Terri died, she gave me a plant. Terri was preparing in her way, and giving me a little life to take care of was a very special gesture, the energy of which has stayed with me ever since. And the energy wasn't all that stayed. That little plant lasted until 2006! It was such a tiny little thing to begin with, but grew bigger and bigger. When I moved to my house in 2003 the lighting was very different and it languished. I tried putting it outside but to no avail, which made me kind of sad. Maybe it was Terri's way of letting me know she was doing just fine in heaven. I looked up one day and told Terri that I thought the plant had had it, and then I blessed it and thanked it for years of reminding me of Terri.

In addition to the plant, Terri had given me a set of four coffee cups decorated with white-robed little-girl angels with crooked halos and bare feet. On one cup above the little angels were the words, "Peace Love and Joy to You." I LOVED IT! That coffee cup is still my favorite cup for coffee. I drink out of it almost every day. I also gave one to my mom, as she was such a support to me during Terri's journey to transition. Terri had a fear of being forgotten, and I remember telling her that she would never be forgotten by me, she's always there every time I fill that coffee cup.

From Terri's journey I learned never to be judgmental; people live and die in all kinds of situations. Terri's situation was rougher than some, and easier than others. Taking care of myself so that I was able to give to another was a valuable lesson I learned during the year I spent with Terri.

As caregivers we sometimes forget that we have to replenish and take care of ourselves to be better prepared to care for others. I have seen many a caregiver go without sleep, or even set foot outside, for days. When we are taking care of someone that is dying we can become consumed with the task of it, and this can be draining. Just doing the little things that you love, like having lunch out with a friend, or slipping away for a couple of hours, will help lighten the load and give the caregiver a fresh start after a challenging day. If you were to compare your body to a car that runs on gas, an empty tank will bring you to a standstill. In working with Terri I learned that I had to create time to replenish and recharge myself in body, mind and spirit.

Chapter 5

Lily, a Harley Girl with Wings

Birth is when I appear out of myself
Life is when I dance within myself
Death is when I disappear into myself.
—Adyashanti

As I write this, I am staring at a card that was given to me by a lovely client called Lily. As I recall the moment Lily gave it to me, my heart skips a little beat—there are no words to describe how I felt when I opened this card. On the front of the card there is a drawing of a woman wearing a long-sleeved, rainbow-colored shirt, grey pants with little red polka dots, and red shoes. Her arms are outstretched and in the middle of her shirt there is a large radiating heart. Above her head in pink is the word YES! Under the right arm are the words, "Excellent Indeed!" Jumping out from under the left arm are the words, "The Best!" And at the very top of the card in lavender and blue it reads, "You really made a difference!" A bright bit of yellow peeps out from the corner of the card, and in the middle, in rainbow letters that feel as if they are vibrating right into my heart are the words, Thanks for your <u>positive energy</u> and <u>total great spirit</u>! The phrases "Total great spirit" and "positive energy," are underlined in pink with little sizzle marks shooting out from the word "energy." And that was just the outside!

The inside of Lily's card states in bold letters, "Consider Yourself Most Appreciated!" Lily had then added her own personal touches—six lipstick kisses after which she wrote, "Can't wait to meet your boyfriend. Maybe he has a friend, ha-ha! We can go riding."

Lily loved Harley Davidson motorcycles.

Last of all, Lily had written, "Thank you so very much for taking care of me. I am so glad I met you. Love, Lily."

Looking at Lily's card always brings back a lot of memories and I have to take a deep breath as I recall the journey I experienced with her.

When I met Lily she was living in a beautiful home with her brother and family. She was in her late 40's and dying of cancer. That first day she was very sick with dry heaves, which continued for the entire visit. So I grabbed the tissues and held the trashcan. She kept apologizing and said that she had gone out the night before, had too much fun and was paying the price. I rubbed her back, told her not to worry and made a joke to ease her mind. I said, "It sucks taking medication! You can't get your groove on!"

Lily had lived in Las Vegas before landing in California for her cancer treatment. After hearing her stories and what her family shared with me, it was clear that Lily been at death's door more than once. I think she may have had nine lives. Lily was also an alcoholic and was trying to get sober. Talk about change! Choosing sobriety and dying at the same time was a reflection of her courage. I was so grateful to be able to be with her during the time that she became clean and clear, and I could see her spirit shine through without the haze of alcohol.

When we first met she was still washing her own clothes and continued to do so for some time. One thing she did that cracked me up was that she used about ten sheets of fabric softener per load. I think that was the only "easier, softer way" Lily was going to experience in this life. At the time I laughed at how many dryer sheets Lily used, but I've discovered that she had a good thing going. I like using a few extra dryer sheets myself now, though not quite so many as she did, and it does make the clothes *so soft*.

Lily took good care of her clothes, and let me tell you, she had a wardrobe that would knock your socks off. This sister believed in having fun and her wardrobe showed it! No matter when I visited she always had on the "sweetest" nightgowns. By sweetest (I am getting the lingo from my twenty year old sons), it means very nice, awesome, and even sexy. And why not? She may have been dying but she was still living as much of her life as she could, and this was something I loved about her. One day we went through her entire wardrobe. She even had shoes that sparkled and lit up. As I helped her in and out of outfits, I learned the history and stories behind each one and it was great fun. It was clear that Lily had lived a fun and full life in Las Vegas. I never asked her but I think she may have been a Vegas showgirl. As the saying goes, what happens in Vegas stays in Vegas! That was fine with me, but my inner wild side was a little bit envious.

Most of the time Lily was fine with her baldness, but she did have some really pretty longhaired wigs that she wore when she went out with her family and friends. She and I only went out one time together, when she asked me to take her to the drug store. Lily was very thin, but "my girl" always dressed up, no matter what. That day she wore a leopard patterned dress and one of her best wigs. It was a hot summer day and she was really craving green apples. So I deposited her at the drug store. She assured me she would be okay, and she told me she would use a motorized cart. I watched her go in to make sure she was able to get a motorized cart before I proceeded to a nearby grocery store to buy her apples. When I returned I discovered Lily was being well taken care of by a sweet lady who had been helping her find everything she needed. I think this is when she bought me the card.

I simply have to go into detail about the handicapped motorized carts provided for customers in some of the larger stores and shopping malls. They are VERY hard to steer, they go fast when they shouldn't, and they slow down in the worst spots. The batteries go dead most of the time. When one is medicated, reverse becomes forward and forward becomes reverse. Crashes occur, people stare, people judge, people scoff, especially if they have almost been hit or maybe bumped. Most people seem to only understand cart incidents when someone is old. If an individual is younger than a senior citizen, and driving one of these contraptions, people are often unbelievably disapproving.

I was glad when our drug store excursion was over, because with the exception of a chosen few, our fellow human beings were just plain rude. I was ready to pounce and declare sternly, "This woman is dying!" But that would be acting like them, and would be rude of me. Lowering yourself is never good for spirit. Fortunately, little words of wisdom bubbled up during my heated moments, calming the lioness in me. *Compassion, Nina. They don't understand,* my heart said. And it's true.

As we sat together each week and talked, I watched Lily open up to her dying process. As Lily as she reviewed her life she realized she had some unfinished business to take care of. She needed more time to die, and that is what she received. When I told Lily I was going on vacation to Florida and would be gone about eight days, to my surprise she said, "I am going on a trip too. I am going to see my grandma." The glimmer I saw in her eyes as she spoke these words told me this was a huge opportunity for goodbyes, closure and healing. She was particularly excited because included in this trip was a "Lily Run." About a hundred Harley's would be riding for Lily in Las Vegas to celebrate her life.

It is a rare occurrence for someone nearing there time to leave hospice to travel! We had to transfer Lily to the hospice where her grandma lived, so they could watch over her there. I helped her pack and discovered Lily's luggage was as interesting and exciting as her wardrobe. Whoa, matching gold and black leopard print—exquisite! I checked our lists to make sure she had everything she needed to make her comfortable, and then she was off on her trip and I left on mine. I said my goodbyes that day, thinking I might never see her again, but deep inside spirit knew better.

When I returned, I felt that it was a miracle that Lily had made it back to California. She had to be hospitalized when she was in Las Vegas, which meant she did not make it to the Harley run. In spite of the fact that things didn't work out the way she had hoped, Lily seemed okay with it all.

She seemed at peace, and I knew it wouldn't be long now. Her body would let go soon.

Surprisingly, Lily lingered. The family was worried and did not understand what was taking so long. Why was she not gone? And as with families in the past, I gently spoke to them about the process of the soul needing to wrap things up in a spiritual sense. What was happening for Lily was that she was fearful about dying and wanted to know, "What's next Nina?" I did the best I could to help ease her mind. All of us at hospice wanted to make this an easy transition for her—so much so that one day, when I was at the house sitting with Lily, we heard a Harley pull up. I couldn't believe it. It was our hospice doctor, and he made her day!

I am going to share with you a little story about Lily that was very difficult for me. Lily's family had asked for a couple who were both preachers at their community church to come over. And as it is with the ways of spirit, my timing was perfect and I was there for her. They were good preachers, and they read some poignant verses to Lily that helped her, and while I was happy to pray with Lily and her family, my senses were keyed into this woman the way a mother is with a child. It was clear to me that Lily was suffering physically, and it seemed no one was paying attention.

We were all standing in a circle as the preacher was finding the perfect verse. Lily was grateful they were there and was being polite to them, though it was clear she was uncomfortable standing. I was starting to get irritated that they weren't looking at her and noticing her discomfort. I watched the preachers thumb through their bibles, so caught up in their Bible verses they didn't notice how Lily kept touching her back and shifting her weight. It was making me very uncomfortable, and I finally looked at the two preachers and said with a bit of authority, "She needs to sit down." I know the preachers meant well, but they weren't hospice chaplains and didn't work around the dying on a daily basis. Hospice Chaplains are very sensitive to the needs of the dying, and it makes a difference in how they handle themselves in such situations!

Once the preachers understood what was wrong, Lily sat and was able to finish her prayers with her family with a little less discomfort. After they left I helped her into bed, and she thanked me. Lily always thanked me. One time she looked straight at me and said, "I can't believe how much you have helped me Nina," It was so heartfelt I cried. I did not feel I had done enough.

I know, I have said this at least once already and will likely say it again and again: Working with the dying is a sacred experience for which I actually thank God over and over again. Being a hospice volunteer has made me sensitive, but not in a bad way at all. It has made me sensitive in a spiritual way—sensing the light and the whispers and feelings of spirit. It is a sensitivity that allows me into a world where many would not be willing to venture. But to me it's an opportunity help others and to use my sixth sense to witness and feel the unseen. I have become more clairsentient, clairaudient and clairvoyant as a result of my time spent with those in transition. What amazing gifts I have received from doing this work! These are gifts that come to me whenever they are needed, that assist me not only with helping with the dying, but also in helping myself and others with all kinds of situations that arise in life.

As I write about Lily I feel her over my right shoulder, helping me find the right words to share her story. She will be waiting for me someday, just like the lady on her card.

On our last day together I couldn't stay long, and Lily insisted on walking me to the door, ignoring my protests, in spite of her weakened state. I didn't realize it was our last day until I stood at the door and our eyes met, and we hugged. She died a few days later escorted peacefully by her loved ones to the other side.

Lily taught me compassion, love and humility. Thank you, Lily.

Chapter 6

Dad and My Biggest Lessons in Life

God grant me the serenity
To except the things I cannot change
The courage to change the things I can
And the wisdom to know the difference.
-Anonymous

As I said before, there can be many gifts in a loss. Such was the case in my journey with my dad's unexpected transition.

As children we had a typical "provider dad." We lived in a nice house, went to good schools, and enjoyed beach and ski vacations. But Dad was never there. He was busy providing these things for us. I do remember that when he was there he made us laugh with his weird antics, singing silly songs with made up words like, takka wakka tunka, words he also liked to use when playing with the dogs. He had such a hearty laugh that I loved to hear. Dad loved Road Runner and Bugs Bunny cartoons too. In essence he was a big kid, and I often think it was because he probably never got to be one himself.

Dad was crazy with the baby powder, and after his shower the entire house would be filled

with the scents of Johnson and Johnson baby
powder and Old Spice cologne. It's such a powerful
memory for me, the smell of the baby powder and
cologne. Dad wore Aramis later on, but for some
reason the Old Spice really has stuck with me, and
when I see the old familiar red package with a ship
on it at the drug store, or a waft of its scent blows
past me from an older gentleman walking by, I
think of my dad.

Another thing I remember so well was
Wednesday nights. When we were young every
Wednesday night Mom, Dad and my three siblings
and I would go out to dinner together as a family.
It was a special time where we all enjoyed Dad's
presence with us. So even though he was busy a
lot, as a child I knew he was my dad just doing
what dads do to take care of their families.

I was not an easy teenager and was often a
wee bit rambunctious at times, testing the waters
as teens do. On top of the mood swings that are
part of teen angst and growth, something
significant took place in my dad's life that changed
his life, and my life, forever: his father died.

I had no idea of the impact a parent's death
can have on an adult child, especially when there is
an unbelievable amount of unfinished business.
When I think back, way back before teenage years,
my dad was kind of tortured in a way, not being
able to be with us on vacations. He was working all
the time, and it was not until much later in my life

that I put together the part that his own father had played in how Dad lived his life.

My dad changed after his father's death. One day Mom said that she felt like Grandpa had *possessed* Dad. I believe she told me that because *something* clearly had changed; Dad became full of anger and indecision. Mom's words made sense. Even though his father was no longer on Earth to demean him or control his life anymore, Dad was left with all the hurts and the unspoken words that that he had held inside since childhood. His father was still there inside of him and Dad was angry about that. And it changed Mom too. One time, Dad took his anger out on me, and I remember Mom just watching. No one could control that kind of rage. I forgave Dad for that incident long ago, because I understood what he was left with after his father passed. But after that incident Mom and Dad's marriage changed, and not in a good way.

Mom left Dad when I was in my late 20's. Dad's response was to disappear inside himself. For years after the divorce he was obsessed with himself and with getting Mom back. Nothing else mattered, not even his kids.

Mom and Dad met when she was eighteen, and were married a year later. They were together a total of 35 years. She was the only girl he ever knew. After they split up, my dad really fell apart. He stalked Mom for years, and he even wanted to take her life at one point. I shudder when I recall the drama and the craziness. I am now blessed with the wisdom to have compassion for the insanity. I understand that the insanity continues if the wound inside is never healed.

I felt angry with my dad, because everything became about Mom where he was concerned. There wasn't room in his life for us kids. He would drive past her house several times a day, and even after the house sold he wrote horrible letters to her. Yearning for peace in her life, Mom moved to Oregon, where she stayed for five years. I missed her so much. With Mom far away, Dad's insanity calmed down a bit, but it didn't last for long. Soon he was back to spreading rumors across the world (we had relatives everywhere), about how Mom had left him. This went on for twenty years.

It took some time, but after a while all the people that Dad had talked to for years about Mom and us, began to realize that he was mentally unstable and suffering from anxiety and depression. Eventually, many family and friends stopped talking to him. As he got older Dad's acquaintances became his only friends, but they were also his angels in disguise. They were restaurant owners, barbers, priests, neighbors, waitresses, bank tellers, and the nameless Armenian lady who made his lunch everyday. These people listened to him. They didn't really know my dad, but somehow I think they understood he needed to be heard.

It was not unusual for Dad to try to use me as a conduit to communicate with Mom. He frequently asked me to go behind her back and give him information, and he even hired private investigators to keep track of her. Dad and I went back and forth for years over his behavior. He would do something terrible, and I would get so mad that I wouldn't speak to him. Like a little kid, he would ask me when he could call me again, and then I would feel bad and forgive him; then it would happen all over again.

What I didn't understand about my dad's erratic and volatile behavior was that it stemmed from abuse he had experienced at the hands of his own father. My dad was horribly verbally abused by his father, right up until his father's death. His father's demeanor was so angry and violent that at the end of my grandfather's life, Dad saw the hospital staff tie him to the bed. I know I'll never forget the day I saw my grandfather in a hospital bed. I had heard from my parents that he was enraged, throwing things, and yelling and screaming at the nurses. He was very angry, and I am sure he was terrified that he was going to die. This was back in the 1970's when hospice was new. Sadly, my grandfather didn't get the help he needed, and neither did my father.

If you think verbal abuse isn't as bad as physical abuse I'm going to ask you to think again. Physical beatings are visible on the body while verbal beatings are not, but both leave deep psychological wounds and can negatively affect a person and all those who love them for a lifetime.

As a child, Dad was not only verbally abused; he was also forced to witness the abuse of his mother. Imagine being a young child, seeing someone you love severely hurt someone else you love, and being powerless to do anything about it. All of this caused my dad to feel completely worthless inside for most of his life. How he learned to carry all of it around with him and survive, I still don't understand. Some days I think he barely survived, though he put up a good front when he was with us as children. We saw the funny, happy dad and had no idea of the inner torture he experienced. When my grandfather died, leaving the issues between he and my dad unresolved and unhealed, Dad was left with a mind, body and spirit wracked with memories of abuse and pain—pain, that eats you up little by little.

Even though I came to understand the reasons Dad behaved the way he did, my compassion for him would ebb and flow. Sometimes the pain was just too much for me. Fortunately, Dad eventually turned to God. He began praying the Rosary several times a day, and went to the Catholic Church every Sunday. Dad prayed for himself, and he prayed for others too. It was clear to me that he had a dark side and a light side. I could see the light side, but his fear and anger often covered it in darkness and did not give him rest until very late in his life. My Dad continued praying because he wanted God to make things right, and I think that ultimately he did experience peace.

This sounds like such a sad story and it is. It's very hard for me to write about, but I think the information is important to share. Family matters can always be uncomfortable but suffering is a choice. I suffered a great deal during my adult years with Dad, and he suffered too. His story is a classic example of a trail of unfinished business. The trail of abuse went even further back in his family history. My grandfather was abandoned by his mother, which filled him with his own pain and affected his life as well as the lives of his children and grandchildren! As the years went by, and Dad continued to refuse to let go of Mom, I felt so much compassion for them both. Mom was the first person to love Dad and he never stopped loving her. He never gave up; he mourned the loss of Mom to the day he died.

Towards the end Mom and Dad lived only a couple of miles from each other, even though they didn't speak. Mom was staying with my sister recovering from cancer treatments, and my brother was finally able to get Dad to move into a senior facility. The facility was beautiful; Dad got used to it and it helped him considerably. When I would make the trip to go see Mom, I would always stop in to check on Dad. We talked about positive things. He said he was sorry for being so hard on me, and I said I was sorry for being so hard on him. I would tell him how much I loved him, with tears in my eyes every time. And when he would regress and start talking about Mom, which always made him sad, I would help him find his way back to the present moment with me.

About a month before Dad died he called to tell me about a very vivid recurring dream he was having of my mom and a baby that looked just like him in it. He said that in the dream Mom was walking down the stairs of my dad's Aunt Zia's house. She handed the baby to my dad and said. "The baby looks like you, Joe."

Of course my dad thought this might have to do with he and my mom getting back together; he never lost hope.

Babies have always meant new beginnings to me in dreams, and I told my dad, "It's a baby, Dad, and it is you, so a new beginning must be coming for you."

A couple of nights later Dad called and said, "Nina, I had the dream again, but this time I was holding the baby and sitting on the couch with my dad."

Again I just said, "Something good is coming Dad." I loved that he had called me about this. It never occurred to me what was coming.

Not long after those dreams Dad fell while getting a suit tailored to wear to visit my mom. He never made that visit; he never made it out of convalescent care. Dad died peacefully at the hospital not really consciously knowing what was happening.

At his funeral I was sad that my dad could not live the life he had wanted to, owing to the fact that there was so much unfinished business his dad had left him with, which rippled into every area of his life. What I do know in my heart is that before he left this earth Dad knew how much his daughter loved him, and I did. My soul was happy about this. Ours was a very important relationship with lessons about forgiveness and love that I needed to learn. There are no words to express the amount of gratitude I have for my dad now.

Death brings up a lot for people, because it is such a life-changing event. Sometimes it pushes us to the edge of what we thought we could cope with. Other times we are more at peace with the death, because the unfinished business has been taken care of. Death also makes us think of our own mortality; getting on with our life, and taking care of ourselves.

I choose to see the gifts in my life that were given to me because of the relationship I had with my dad—compassion for others' pain, and the behaviors caused by that pain, forgiving those for the pain they have caused me and others, and, of course, forgiving myself for my part in things. The wisdom in all of this is in knowing there was, and always is, a divine plan in everything that God

places in front of us. The final gift I credit to my
father is that I made a decision that the painful
trail of unfinished business was stopping with me.

I feel like my dad understood the gift he left
me with and I still feel his presence even though
he has passed into the next life. When I was living
in Australia I felt him frequently. I was very much
alone there, and several times Dad came to me, sat
on the bed, stroked my hair, or just softly spoke
some comforting words that I don't remember. I
would always wake up smiling and feeling better.
Now I feel his presence all the time in a special
tree outside my garage. It's a quiet place that I
walk past everyday, and when I pass by he gets my
attention in the whispers of the leaves. I feel that
in heaven Dad has the freedom now to be the
supportive father he always wanted to be.

Chapter 7

"Leaving Ego Nina in the Car

"If you Judge people you have no time to love them."
—Mother Teresa

I once read somewhere that a good hospice volunteer leaves everything they know in the car. It may sound funny, but it's true. We all have thoughts and insights about things, but it is important to remember to leave judgment aside and become a blank page when working with the terminally ill. I have to be a blank page when I walk into a private home or a skilled nursing facility so that I can be fully open to whatever I may encounter.

When I walked into Lily's house I found her throwing up after a night on the town. Estelle, on the other hand, greeted me at the door with the words: "I have missed you, and I am glad we can be together for this part of the journey!"

Being a blank page means being open to new experiences and new ways of thinking, and also accepting, allowing, and respecting old ways of thinking. It's important to leave *me* in the car so I can set aside my own personal judgments to whatever I may find. Challenging? Yes it is. This is called "present moment practice" folks.

Typically, when hospice assigns us a patient, we receive a short overview of the patient, their age, marital status, details about their illness, and information about the family members present in the home, and so on. After thoroughly evaluating this, I make my first phone call to the assigned family member, and the relationships begins right there on the phone with that initial contact. Most of the time love is present, and family and friends are helpful. But every now and then there are situations where I feel family members are unfair to the patient, or I get a little uncomfortable with the way a patient is being treated. Of course, if the patient is in danger physically my inner lioness comes out and I have no problem speaking up and advocating for their safety.

I always keep in mind that it is not my journey of death; it is theirs. As long as I leave Nina in the car I can allow "something bigger" to take place. Maybe a better word for "something bigger" could be "allowing."

God's next assignment was a tough one for me. All my patients are divinely partnered, and such was the case with James. I just wanted to scoop him up in my arms and tell him how loved he was. While I was working with James and his family I had to do a lot of "allowing" and ego Nina had to sit in the car a great deal of the time.

Spirit tapped me on the shoulder and whispered in my ear that this man had a life filled with many stories long before I appeared, and in that precious moment a great love washed over me. By being able to leave Nina in the car and set my judgments aside, I was able to avoid all the worry and relentless effort to figure out how to bring more love into James's life, and do my best to resolve any pain that he might have experienced over the previous 80 years. It was a good thing, because every time I went to James's house I was faced with frustrating situations, particularly when I had encounters with his son Derek.

Derek was really struggling with the death of his father, and his discomfort permeated the house in a variety of ways. Derek's house was on the edge of a beautiful golf course. It was summertime, and outside the birds were singing and flowers were blooming. But the blinds in the house were always drawn. Derek did not want to let the light in even though he was not there most of the time. I really wanted to talk with him, but it was difficult for him to make eye contact with me. He was just "not there yet." No eye contact means, "Please don't speak with me, this is too much for me to handle." Derek worked a lot, and this was how he dealt with his father's transition. As I said earlier, I had to set aside judgment. It was his journey, not mine. I was only with this family four months while Derek had experienced a lifetime with his dad.

The caregivers, of which James had experienced many, had been treated without respect while they did everything from cleaning up James, to grocery shopping, laundry, cooking, cleaning the cat box, and often sleeping on the floor next to him. They were exhausted every time I visited, and a couple of them told me they didn't like being there, but they needed their jobs. It was so sad, and I just listened but didn't comment. My experience with hospice has always been with nurses, social workers, doctors, staff and volunteers who love what they do, so this situation was rare for me. I love my job, and I am aware that many may not feel the same way about working with hospice patients as I do. Some do it to pay the bills, not because they love the work.

The thoughts that entered my mind were so difficult to control. Words of judgment about everyone involved with James would creep up out of nowhere. I kept feeling like the son was more interested in the free help than in his dad's dying process. At times that really was what it felt like. But it wasn't my right to make a judgment about it. It was just my brain, my ego, trying to say, "Nina, we know what's best for this family. Let's do something!" Wrong. Wrong. Wrong! See why I leave her in the car? The higher purpose of James's plan was unfolding exactly as it should, in spite of what I might have thought about it.

Here's God's way. The son walks in, treats the care givers coldly, makes no eye contact with me, barely speaks with or makes eye contact with his dad, either. I had to truly quiet my mind and observe to see that God was present there. He always is. With this realization and a deep breath, my personality and ego were left behind. The question was, "What would love do?" Beautiful! Wonderful! Immediately Nina was off the hook. This was love's job not mine.

Mother Teresa said, "In this life we cannot do great things, we can only do small things with great love." Many, many things happened at James's house that challenged me to BE love in everything I did. That word is special too; because I was no longer *doing* with James, I was now able to *be* with him. As a result of just being present with James I was more tuned in, aware and better able to assist him with the unconditional love I could offer. James wasn't the only one to benefit. His son, his caregivers, even the energy of the house benefited from my being able to just be love. Each time I left, I felt as if I was leaving a trail of sparkles and light behind.

On one occasion, I was in a situation where I was going to have to miss seeing James, because I had another commitment at the time I normally saw him. Something told me to forget the other commitment and go. When I arrived I discovered James had thrown up and the caregivers had just finished cleaning him up. We were standing there looking at James when he threw up again. I grabbed some gloves and helped James's tiny caregiver, Tink, with a second cleanup. She would get so flustered when James threw up. She told me, "I am terrible when people throw up. I cry when I throw up!"

"Me too," I said. In the middle of all this, James, who was listening to us, rolled his eyes in a joking way. He was trying to be a good sport with a sense of humor in a less than pleasant situation, and we experienced a moment of hilarity in the midst of mucky chaos as we put James to rights again, only to have him throw up a third time.

When we finally got James to the point that he stopped heaving and was once again clean I sat with him and rubbed his head until he fell asleep.

After he was asleep Tink walked me to the door, and said, "So you are support, right?"

"Yes, I am a volunteer. I am here for support." I replied.

Tink's jaw dropped. She could not believe I was not paid, and I explained to her that hospice was my calling and I shared how long I had been doing hospice work. I also told her that my other job is as an intuitive healer. She looked up at me and said, "Nina, I just knew there was something about you!"

It made me smile. I then told her that I lived just up the street, that I knew she was alone most of the time at James's house, and if she were ever waiting for hospice to arrive and got scared, she could call me and I would come as soon as I could. Before I left that day I asked Tink if there was anything else she wanted or needed. She asked for a hug, and I gave her the best and most healing hug I could muster.

When I made my last visit to James, I could sense that his time was very near, and his room was becoming crowded with unseen loved ones who were coming together to gather him up and take him *Home*.

I was so pleased when I arrived to see that Lucy, one of my favorite caregivers, was looking after James. She was the only one who had known James before he became a hospice patient. She wasn't just a caregiver; she and James were friends. On this particular day she was wearing a Pooh Bear shirt, that said something like "love is all around," with Pooh rolling around on his back. The doorbell rang and it was Jenny, another nurse from hospice whom I loved. So three very special women were in the departure room with James that day.

James was running a high fever and Jenny was trying to bring it down fast. The only way at this stage in James's illness that this could be done was with a Tylenol suppository. James had to be moved, and Jenny did her best to make him as comfortable as possible while she dispensed his medication, and then took time to gently and carefully clean him. James was frustrated with all the moving and cleaning so I stroked his hair and held his hand as Jenny and Lucy worked quickly to get him comfortable.

I watched every little movement made by these two compassionate women, my senses were heightened, and I was on sacred ground. Lucy responded to every little groan James made. "I know honey, I know," she would say.

It is important when someone is "ready" to create a sacred space for them by turning off the TV, playing calm, soothing "light" music in the background, and keeping the room quiet and comfortable. We all knew James was close. The hospice nurse turned down the TV, combed his hair because she knew that James found this soothing, and signaled that we should talk quietly.. I gave James Reiki and whispered to him, "You're going home soon my friend, don't be afraid, it will all be okay." And I kissed his head when I said goodbye, knowing I would not see him again. I am so glad I gave him that kiss.

James died peacefully three days later. I will be forever grateful to this lovely man who helped me learn to leave *ego* Nina in the car and just BE love.

Chapter 8

Hazel's Gaze

"The light of the body is the eye: if therefore thine eye be single, thy whole body shall be full of light."
Mathew 6:22 KJV (King James Version)

Hazel was an egg farmer. She had raised chickens, collected their eggs and delivered them, until she was simply no longer able to physically do it anymore. She had the look of a farmer, too—tall and strong in appearance with a simple and beautiful face, weathered from her years spent outdoors. When I met Hazel she was living in a senior assisted living facility. When I arrived for my first visit with Hazel the home health aide gently lifted the blanket covering her legs to expose her very large and swollen feet. The assisted living facility staff were doing their best to help her, but nothing would fit on her feet, not even the biggest men's slippers or the largest pair of socks, so she spent her days and nights completely barefoot.

Hazel sat in her big chair all day and slept in it at night, as she was very uncomfortable in her bed. She felt better when she was in her chair, and being around others probably made her feel better too. In fact, throughout our time together the only time, I saw her out of that chair was when we put her in a wheel chair and rolled her to the kitchen table for a meal. The other six residents cheered as Hazel pulled up to the table for lunch! She lit up when all the others applauded, and they were happy to have her at the table. For me, it was a tender and beautiful moment. I had a big lump in my throat as I beamed a 'thank you' to God for the opportunity to witness this kind of thoughtfulness.

There was a married couple at the table that day, and the husband clapped the loudest when Hazel made it to the table. He transitioned one day shortly after, and his wife became very sad, scared and fearful without him. I would rub her shoulders and try to comfort her, but without him she was lost. It was clear that she was declining quickly after his passing and would join him soon.

The assisted living center was loud. Either the news or a soap opera was always blaring when I would arrive, because several other women were usually on the couch watching TV, and their hearing was not so good. This made it difficult to talk with Hazel, but we made the best of it, shaking our heads at what we were seeing.

I planned my visits at lunchtime so I could help Hazel eat. She had a daughter in-law, Mary, who also came to visit her often. On one of my visits Mary and I happened to be there. She was glad to see me and shared with me about Hazel's decline over the last year. Mary was concerned about Hazel living at the assisted living facility. She needed reassurance that Hazel wasn't lonely and that she was being properly cared for. She explained that it had become difficult to take care of Hazel at home, and the family had to make the agonizing decision to move her to the assisted living facility. Most families end up doing this if work schedules prevent the family from being able to provide adequate care at home.

As Hazel's health deteriorated I noticed that she gazed at me a lot. We would sit together and watch some dumb soap opera, and I would look over at her and she would be gazing at me. It was not a stare it was a gaze. It was as if she was gazing right through me and into my soul. It didn't feel creepy, or weird. But when it happened I felt a great love wash over me. During the holidays Hazel and I spent a great deal of time together. We exchanged recipes, and she shared her favorite memories about past holidays—what she had cooked and who had come over. I think it was a wonderful time for both of us as we continued to bond and build a relationship.

Hazel's dying process began to accelerate around the same time the assisted living facility started having some issues with the other patients, It was very strange. The situations that arose reminded me of how when one baby cries all the others begin to cry too. At this particular board and care it felt like everyone was feeling everyone else's pain.

As different scenarios played out at the board and care, I think Hazel must have watched me more than I knew. There was another woman who was often in the same room with us, and she was in pain. The caregivers seemed frustrated because all their efforts to get her to lie still and to make her comfortable were to no avail. It was hard for me to witness, and I went over to rub her back. She looked so worried—clearly something was going on inside her. I was glad I could give comfort and love to her, and I know it helped in some way. Then one day she wasn't there, and I found out they had taken her to the hospital one night and she had died quickly from something that happened in her brain. The caregivers did not know all the details, but it was enough to know that she had died quickly. I was relieved she was out of pain and at peace.

To this day I think *my girl* Hazel saw something in me or around me, because during our last visits she gazed and I would gaze back. I felt that Hazel was looking into my soul.
It was like we met in another place and time for brief moments, and it was good

Many years ago I used to Sufi dance. Before the dance begins you *connect* with your partner through eye gazing. Partners are exchanged as we dance around the circle, and making that connection and holding the gazes through the dances is uplifting and wonderful. I remember the different *feel* of each person I gazed at during the dance. The facilitator told me that when we eye-gaze what takes place is the God in me sees the God in you. So simple, and it was true! I loved learning to eye-gaze.

I challenge you to try an eye-gazing experiment of your own. Break out the soft soothing music (like massage music or something of that nature), light some candles, and create a safe and peaceful environment around you. Invite the divine celestials into your space too, they like it! Then eye-gaze with someone you love. Gaze deeply into the other person's eyes for one minute. Even if it feels odd, just relax into it. You won't believe what a wonderful and amazing experience you will have.

Chapter 9
Finding Peace in Grief

The sea is mightier than any river,
yet the sea lies below any river,
is open to any river,
The survivor is the sea of love.

There might be an angry, rushing river.
There might be a lazy tired river.
There might be a crooked, treacherous river.
There might be a polluted river.

The sea is open to them all.
The sea receives them all.
They are transformed in the sea.
Because the sea allows them to transform
The survivor is a sea of love.
—Douglas Cory Smith

While sitting on my patio enjoying the early evening, I caught a glimpse of a little lime-colored green worm that was stuck in a spider web. The web was very close to the ground and the worm was not far from safety. I watched the worm struggling so hard to break free from the web that he just became even more entangled. If a worm could panic it sure seemed like that's what this one was doing. The harder he struggled the deeper in trouble he became. He needed help. I realized that if I intervened he would have a second chance at life. It would just take a little nudge to get him out of the web, and safety was so close! In fact it was just beneath him, inches away, which to a little tiny green worm was probably a great distance!

You probably know where I am headed with this story about my little green friend . . . As I watched him I thought of how like us that little worm was. . When we get stuck—and I mean scary stuck—we need a loving soul to come along and help us out of the web we've tangled ourselves up in. Sometimes all it takes is just a little nudge or tug.

I reached down and helped release the tiny worm from his silken prison and placed him on the ground. Now it was up to him to keep going. It takes strength to keep moving forward, and for the worm a little tiny puddle of water nearby could spell death. He must have sensed this because he changed direction and started to move around it. He wanted to live.

Maybe the moral of this little story is that in life we are never alone, whether we are a little green worm or a human being. When we are stuck Spirit will send someone to help us. But from there it is up to us to choose to live, to use our discernment, and to find our peace.

Dearly Departed: What I Learned About
Living from the Dying

After I brought our little tiny friend to safety it was difficult watching him struggle through the puddles and the big leaves he needed to get through, but if I had rescued him every time he came upon an obstacle, he would have learned nothing. The same goes for all of us. We don't need to be rescued at every turn. And we don't need to go around trying to save everyone around us, either. But a nudge and loving support when needed can empower family, friends, neighbors, coworkers or whoever crosses your path. Help them to help themselves so that they may learn and grow.

The worm story is also a metaphor for events that happen in life that shake us to the core, or pull the rug out from under our feet. We have all experienced extreme sadness, anger, or frustration that can make life seem unbearable. This is when people come into our life for a reason, a season or a lifetime, as the saying goes. Often they are not there for our lifetime, but are with us only for a while to help us in our time of need. They are God's earth angels.

I am an earth angel to many. And many times when tragedy happens, I nudge, I love, I empower, and then they leave "my house." I pray for them, and sometimes it can be challenging for me to let them leave.

I met Wendy at an event where I was giving healings. Wendy had just moved to California from the Midwest. Her brother had committed suicide only three months before, and they were very close. I felt her pain as her eyes searched mine for answers. Her life felt like it was unraveling. She felt as though she was being swept downstream and there were no branches to reach for. I tried to schedule time with her, because I could see how badly she needed it. But she refused, saying she just could not come if she could not pay me, and her job didn't start for another four weeks.

Since she wouldn't schedule sessions with me we talked on the phone instead. Even on the phone I could tune into her and feel her pain, and I was provided with just the right words to say. I don't think any one person can give you peace. We need to find it within ourselves, but a little help along the way can be good. Over several conversations I was able to help Wendy find ways to achieve a sense of balance and peace in her life.

There are some tools you can use when you need to turn within to find your peace that can help you achieve that same sense of peace and balance that Wendy so desperately needed. This is done through adjusting your frequency, or vibration, and there are a number of ways to do this. One way is through simple meditation techniques. Here's an example of a meditation I use all the time:

1.) Start with a four-count breath, breathing in to a slow count of four, and

breathing out to a slow count of four. If it is
difficult to breath through your nose, do
what's comfortable. The key is a nice deep
breath that starts deep in the belly. Expand
the belly like a balloon as you breathe in (it
helps to rest your hand on your belly so you
can feel it). Let your belly relax into the
breath, and then bring the breath up to your
chest. You will find your breathing much
deeper. Give it a try while you're here now
reading this, three times. Breathe in through
the nose slowly, 1 ... 2 ... 3 ... 4 ... and out
through the nose 1 ... 2 ... 3 ... 4 ...

2.) Next I want you to think about the
ocean, sitting on the beach. The continuous
ebb and flow of the great ocean is a
wonderful symbol for using sound and
rhythm for the breath. When watching the
waves at the shore, they pull back and then
they roll in. As the waves pull back into the
ocean, that's your breath in. When the waves
roll up onto the shore, creeping higher and
higher onto the sand, that's your breath out.
If any thoughts float into your mind, just let
them float on by and allow them to flow
gently into the ocean.

3.) Last but not least bring the ocean into
your body and really *feel* it. Bring all your

senses to bear in bringing the ocean into your body. When you breathe in, feel the ocean waters being drawn all the way up your spine. Start at the base and breathe in all the way up to the top of your head. Then as you breathe out, let the water, and sounds cascade down the front of your body.

You have just meditated. This simple meditation technique can be done for long or short periods of time, focusing on the breath to calm the mind chatter, which is one of the main points of the meditation, with the mother ocean as your guide. Even just a few minutes doing this little meditation will help you feel calmer and . Believe me, I know this can be an effort when you are very sad (or angry, fearful, frustrated, etc.,), but give it a try anyway. Just breathe and focus on the breath. The breath brings you into the present moment. Mind chatter cannot reside in the present moment.

Music is another way to shift your vibration and calm your thoughts—not music that has lots of words, though. We want to calm the mind chatter. Look for music that is soothing, instrumental, ambient, or nature sounds. The important thing is that it *not* have lyrics and that it be pleasant and comforting to listen to. Using a headset to listen to music is a good idea, especially if you're using the breathing technique. Keep soothing music on wherever you are, in the car, at the office, or at home. It will help you clear away the mind clutter, and when the mind chatter stops your vibration rises.

There is no greater example of being in the present moment than when you observe nature. Get outside and "be" with the nature around you. Pay attention to what you see, hear, smell, taste and touch. Walk in it, dig in it, water it, sit in it, feel it under your toes, breath it in, let its energy encompass you. Allow nature to take you onto a healing journey of spirit. If you can manage it, try to find longer periods of time to devote to nature. Maybe you can take a long hike, or even enjoy a weekend away in a natural setting. But if you can't get away for long, don't worry. Nature is right outside your door. Even ten minutes caring for plants, digging, or just sitting with a cup of coffee watching the local wildlife and insects will do.

I was having lunch with one of my girlfriends who was having a hard day. As we were saying goodbye, she slipped her shoes off and put her bare feet in the grass. Her face completely changed as soon as her toes hit the grass! Ahhh! I saw the grass poking up in between her toes, and I thought how cool it must have felt. I looked at her and smiled. What a great idea!! So simple, and when you do something like that it brings you into the present moment. It's a *feel good* moment, and for that present moment everything else is forgotten. Our vibration is raised, inner smile intact.

Grief shows up in our life at many different times and not just with death. Elizabeth Kubler-Ross's model of the five stages of grief can be helpful to refer to when you or a loved one are struggling with the journey through grief. Notice I say through, because grief can never ever be walked around. You have to move through it, as it will reappear when you least expect it.

The five stages of grief are denial, anger, bargaining, depression and acceptance. These stages can overlap, intermingle, and sometimes we may move back and forth between them, But we do all seem to experience them as we move through grief, though each person's experience is unique. If you are able to prepare for the death of a loved one it makes the process a little easier. Anticipatory Grief is a term used to describe preparing for the death of another person. I am not sure HOW much easier it makes it on us. Maybe it just puts us a little ahead in the process by the time it happens, though I don't think anything could have prepared me for the loss of my mother. Knowledge may help prepare the mind, but the heart is an essence and energy that we have no control over.

Whether we get the chance to prepare or not, especially with sudden death as in suicide, or a sudden terminal illness that moves very quickly, grief comes, and having support is a must. In preparing for my own mom's passing I discovered that what others say and what I know comes from the heart: grief comes in waves, some days they crash and other days they are just lapping at the shore.

I run into people all the time who, especially if I am wearing my hospice badge, want to talk about an experience they had. Rarely have I heard that someone had a bad experience with hospice. People always tell me how wonderful the hospice team was to them and how they helped them with their mom, dad, grandma, and grandpa. They always bless me and thank me for doing the work I do, and I sense these folks are doing okay with their grief process at that moment in time. Then there are others, where time has gone by and they say to me, "It's been a year. I should be doing better."

My first words to them are always, "You get to take as much time as you need. There is no set time to grieve. There is no being done or finished with grieving. Over the years its gets a little easier, that's all."

Chapter 10

A True Blue Walmart Shopper

"Be who you are and say what you feel . . .
Because those that matter . . .
don't mind . . .
And those that mind . . .
don't matter."
—Dr. Seuss

Louise was a real gem of a patient who, in her
mind, was still far from departing this earth. I have
to tell you, this woman made me laugh so much.
She had a way about her and carried herself with
such determination. She commanded respect and
held her head high, and when she spoke I listened.
I honored every bit of her journey and was glad to
be a part of it.

After living in New Jersey her entire life,
Louise arrived in Temecula with her daughter,
Anna, and granddaughter. The three of them had
lived together in New Jersey, and had come to
California to move in with her son and his lovely
family because of Louise's cancer.

It was clear that Louise had already
experienced great loss from having to move away
from all her friends and everything she was

familiar with. It was a big change for her, and it
was made even harder because her son lived on
the east end of Temecula, which was rather
isolated at the time Louise was living there. Public
transportation in Temecula was not at all like it
had been in New Jersey, where one could hop on a
bus and go just about anywhere. A relatively new
community, Temecula was considered to be rural;
there were few bus routes and busses were
infrequent. Louise was used to getting out and
about and this was frustrating for her because it
made her feel isolated and left her dependent on
others to get around town.

When I arrived at their house for the first
time, I stood at the front door waiting for some
time and suddenly heard a loud crash! I thought,
*oh my goodness, my patient has fallen! Is she in
there alone?* I called through the door, "Are you
okay?"

The voice coming back sounded younger
than I expected, and when the door opened I was
greeted by a woman in her early 40's who could
barely walk. It was Louise's daughter Anna who
was suffering with Multiple Sclerosis. Immediately
in my mind I considered the concerns Louise must
have had about leaving behind a handicapped
daughter and young granddaughter.

Louise came down the stairs with a smile on
her face and seemed genuinely pleased to meet
me. The next thing I knew we were off on a

shopping trip to Walmart. I had never conducted this kind of excursion with a hospice client before. I'm not particularly fond of visiting Walmart as I find it overwhelming—the monster parking lot, the long aisles, and the throngs of people. I feel the same about Costco. My preference is for smaller places. Over the next two months, Louise and I visited Walmart every week, except one.

Louise had a very dry sense of humor, which I thoroughly enjoyed. I would laugh so much with her. She also loved new babies. Whenever she saw little ones her face would light up, and she always stopped and talked to mothers. Louise was also a Southern Baptist, and Lord would it ever come out sometimes, which I respected completely, of course. She had strong beliefs about appropriate child rearing, and when she would see someone not minding their children she would say, "Lord (pronounced Laaaud), Nina. I should not talk like this about other people, but what is wrong with those parents?" Spending time with Louise was always entertaining.

Louise was in denial about dying when I met her. She was an active person, and said she felt good. So, although her cancer was there, we pretended it wasn't, or that she had been misdiagnosed. That was what she needed and wanted to believe, and my job was to validate her feelings and keep my heart open for her with no preconceived ideas or judgments. Since Louise and I were always driving somewhere, I could not leave ego Nina in the car, so I had to leave ego Nina at home.

My intuition told me that despite the brave face Louise showed to the world, she was afraid. She hadn't planned on this happening to her, and I felt it in a big way—an energy that hung thick in the air. Early on in our relationship I had a profound dream that changed my life. I now know what it "feels" like to not be ready to die. I woke up crying from the dream and said to my then husband that I had died and had found myself at the gates of Heaven. I was standing at a door that was open and I could see a long hallway. A beautiful shorthaired lady (she is an angel that has been in many of my dreams) was standing at the door. I looked at her and said, "Can I go in and then come out?"

She practically twinkled as she looked at me and replied, "No, once you go in you cannot go back."

"But I need to go find my sister," I said, feeling a sense of panic. At this point my angel friend understood. I turned around to go find my sister and behind me were lots of other people sitting at tables working on their unfinished business! I then woke up.

It took me some time to realize that this dream was not about me. I was feeling all of Louise's "stuff" and there was lots of it. I believe the panic I felt in my dream was because, at that time, I had not talked to my sister and could not imagine leaving the earth without saying goodbye and telling her I loved her. I thought *Louise has to leave a handicapped daughter, her grandchildren, son and other family members along with her close friends she left in New York. That's a lot when you aren't ready.* I don't know if anyone is ever ready when we must leave people we love behind. This is why it is so important to smile a lot, to forgive, and to not hold out on the "I love you's." It just may make it a little easier when it's time to make the journey home.

The importance of Walmart for Louise was familiarity and purpose. Walmart shopping was a familiar activity, and driving Miss Louise there every week gave her a sense of purpose, because it provided her with an opportunity to contribute to the family.

There were certain items that were very important to Louise—lotions, sheets and towels. I knew she was trying to make her new space comfortable, and we would stand for hours talking about what sheets to buy, or trying to decide which lotion made her skin feel the softest. Louise was a diabetic with a powerful sweet tooth, and Walmart sold single-serving pies in every flavor you could think of, which Louise could never resist. After finding the items she needed she would also buy dinner for the family as well as necessities for Anna and her granddaughter, Kiya, like body washes, razors and school clothes. Our lunch was always a Chinese take-out from Panda Express--five fried shrimp and a soda, which I would get and we would eat in the car.

I could feel how important shopping was to Louise, and was always happy to take as long as she needed. Each Walmart trip was normally a four-hour visit. On one of my shopping trips with Louise I bought a dress that I wore all that summer. Under Louise's tutelage I was growing into a Walmart shopper.

My funniest Walmart adventure with Louise happened one day when she needed bras. If you have ever bought a bra at Walmart you may already know that they have really large sizes, like 50DD even. When I saw such large bra sizes I said, "Oh my gosh, Louise. I would not know what to do if I had all that?"

She replied, "Ummm hmmm, bet her man is saying, 'Come to daddy!'" I laughed so hard at her comments. Most of the time they would come out of nowhere and catch me completely off guard. Louise had a great sense of humor.

As Louise's cancer progressed I noticed that she would be a little bit more medicated each time I picked her up. Medication and electric carts are not a good combo, and one day Louise got confused about the controls on the cart—her forward became reverse and reverse became forward—and before she knew it she had actually pinned an employee in the chip aisle. I tried to assist her in backing up, which confused her even more. One more wrong move and the poor girl would not be able to breathe! Just as the young woman let out a squeal, more from fear than pain, Louise and I were able to release her. Fortunately she was very kind and understanding about the whole situation, as she could see Louise's struggle.

"I'm sorry," Louise said as we backed her up as fast as we could. Thankfully, no harm was done that day. However the same cannot be said for a number of displays that were unceremoniously mown down. And Louise definitely added her fair share of dings and scrapes to ye ole' "electro-mobile."

I shared a lot about my adventures with Louise with my mom, and I asked her if she wanted to join us sometime on one of our trips. When she finally did accompany us, Mom said I had lots of patience, and it was true. For one thing, Louise never wanted me to assist her. She would have nothing to do with holding hands, guiding elbows, nothing! When she would teeter sometimes and I would unconsciously raise a hand to steady her, she would say loud and clear, and a bit sassy, "Nina, I don't need your help. Don't touch me." Of course, I would explain to her that I couldn't have her falling on my watch, but it didn't change a thing.

The day Mom was with us we also went to The Dollar Store across from Walmart. The Dollar Store had no electric carts, so I dropped Mom and

Louise off at the door and went to park the car.
When I looked back there they were, walking into
the store together, arms intertwined like
girlfriends. Louise needed a girlfriend her age, and
it was so sweet to watch the two of them together.

Sadly, it wasn't long before Louise's health
deteriorated to the point where we could not do
any side shopping at The Dollar Store or the 99
Cents Only stores, if they did not have carts she
couldn't make it.

For about four visits I was driving a big six-
wheel truck to see her. I would hold my breath
until her butt was safely parked in the front seat
and she was buckled in. She would look over at
me, smile and say, "It ain't no big thing, Nina."

Many times we would have to wait for
electric carts at Walmart, and sometimes we'd take
a seat for as long as 20 minutes. Louise and I
would wonder where all the carts were. *How sick
were those other people? How come they couldn't
walk?* One day I learned a big lesson about making
judgments . . . Louise and I were waiting next to
another lady who was getting a cart before us. She
was a big girl and not very old at all, and Louise
was just as curious as I was about why she didn't
walk through the store and exercise her body.

Louise and I respectfully asked the young
woman what happened to her. She then explained
in detail how she had fallen on the job when she
was working as a nurse. Her ankle had never

healed properly, and consequently she'd gained a lot of weight and couldn't walk or exercise. She would never have been able to shop at Walmart without those carts. At Walmart I learned not to judge who should be using carts, just based on appearances. Apparently I needed to leave *ego* Nina in the car when I went to Walmart, too!

Are you up for an experiment? Go to a place like Walmart and see how spiritual you can be as you watch and interact with people. Try to BE LOVE. Walk through that store and bless everyone, the regular shoppers, the electric cart shoppers, employees, happy and unhappy children, happy people, angry people, inconsiderate people, and people who are lost. It's possible you may find it a bit hard at first, but I guarantee you'll be a better person for it, because when you bless and love others you are blessing and loving yourself too. The Buddha says we are all one, and when you bless people instead of chasing those thoughts of who, what, or why, it will lift you up into a state of love. We are all trying to get there safely.

I'm grateful to Louise, for helping me to be a better person and a better Walmart shopper. I can't help but smile big every time I think of her.

Chapter 11

Still Alive at Ninety-Five

Your age brings me comfort
A life that has been fully lived
So blessed I am to be in this presence
Beautiful light you are
Go in peace on your journey home
Until we meet again . . .
—Nina

Margie came into my life, just as another of my patient's life was coming to a close. Taking on two patients at a time is something I had never done, but my intuition told me that all would be well. My last patient's process had taken its toll on me, and normally I would just take a break, but when I met Margie and her wonderful daughter and son-in-law they were such a breath of fresh air I knew I had made the right decision. The family lived in the beautiful wine country in the Temecula Valley, so the drive alone, to visit their home, was so peaceful.

Margie was 95 and had congestive heart failure. The family had requested an "as needed" volunteer, which meant that visits were supposed to be non-frequent i.e., every couple of weeks or so. Many times when the family requests volunteers on an "as needed" basis they quickly learn how lovely it is not only for them, but also for the care of the patient. It wasn't long before I was seeing Margie on a regular basis.

When I met Margie for the first time I was amazed at her clarity and independence, as well as her candidness about her dying process. "So, do you just sit with people?" She asked me.

"Yes." I smiled.

Then she said, "You know, I had an encounter."

"Oh," I responded with a compassionate nod. She began to explain to me that she believed that she had died the previous week and had gone up to God. She spoke slowly, explaining to me the feeling of her heart stopping and then the sensation of floating. Margie made it clear that she knew she had died for just a moment. Then she looked me right in the eye and said, "Then my heart started back up again and I came back to my body." She said she was not scared and was ready to go whenever God felt it was time.

Margie enjoyed my visit so much that day, and since it was obvious to me that she had enjoyed an active social life, I called her daughter the following week and asked if I could visit Margie every week. She was more than pleased.

At 95 years of age, just about everyone Margie knew had already died, and I knew it made her sad. She told me that sometimes she would lie in bed and think of people she had not thought about in years. My sense is that this IS an integral part of the dying process. Moreover, I have good reason to believe that all those friends and family who have gone before us often are standing around the bed of a loved one who is about to pass. I have personally felt their presence on many occasions, and have witnessed patients talking to loved ones only they can see . I believe that when death approaches, the veil between this world and the next becomes much thinner, enabling those who care about us to come close enough for us to be aware of them on some level. I believe this was why Margie was thinking of all those folks from her past. Perhaps they were right there with her, joyfully awaiting her arrival on the other side. This is very akin to the feeling of excitement over the arrival of a new baby. We learn about the stages of pregnancy and anticipate the birth, pondering the mystery and miracle of it all. In preparing for birth we want the baby to be comfortable and feel nurtured, so we buy baby things, read books about child birth and infant care, and prepare the nursery. There is much anticipation about the coming event and what it will be like. For example, will it be painful? Will the new baby be okay? Are we doing everything we can to make sure the mother is getting enough rest and is not under too much stress?

Just as with preparations for birth there is a similarity in how we can choose to prepare for death. First we get the initial news of how much time we have, then we begin to learn everything we can about what's happening to us, and we start to prepare ourselves and our families: this is a very important time of learning. We want to know if it will be painful, will we (or our loved one) be okay, and will the transition be stressful? Dying is a rebirth into the next life, and with it there is so much mystery. But the miracle in death is that it's not an end; it's just a transition. Margie was preparing to be birthed into her next life and her friends and family who had gone before her were waiting to welcome her to her new life.

Before Margie moved in with her daughter and son-in-law she had lived in Phoenix, where she was very active in The Church of Christ. I sensed that she missed this kind of community. She had found another Church of Christ in a nearby town, but when she became sick and could not leave the house to go to church, her connections with her church community became less frequent. People get busy and wine country is way out there for some, so she didn't get many visits from other church members. This was hard for Margie and she frequently reminisced about her church, Bible studies, potlucks and special friends. She missed her social life tremendously. I mentioned to her that hospice had spiritual care and that they would come to visit her whenever she liked. Soon spiritual care was coming once a week. It wasn't like her own church but the chaplains were very caring and sweet and brought her both comfort and the spiritual connection with others that was missing from her life.

On one particular day that I visited Margie I noticed she seemed weak and did not have her usual spark. Her daughter had run to the store, and Margie and I were alone. She seemed as if she was trying to doze off but her breathing was very labored, and I had the sense that she was worried or anxious. As I watched her, the thought flitted through my mind that she could die anytime. Margie interrupted that thought by asking me to read from the Bible. She knew the Bible well, and found its words very comforting..

"Pick any chapter you want." Margie said.

It was a VERY old Bible and I did my best. I was glad to see that my Bible reading had a soothing effect on her. When I paused for a minute, she looked up at me and said I had a wonderful voice—that it was a calling. I pulled her hand into mine and thanked her. I don't know if I'll be called upon to read the Bible to others or not, but I'm glad I was willing to do this for Margie, as it was clear that the passages I read were very comforting to her. In hospice I make it a point to always be mindful and sensitive. My feelers are always up!

Many times at this stage of the process a patient will have a catheter to collect urine so they don't have to get up. Not Margie! She would grab her walker and scoot over to the bathroom. As I walked with her I would sometimes gently touch her back, and notice how tiny, frail and crooked it had become over her many years. We'd get close to the potty, and I would help her with her nightgown. Call me crazy but helping a dying person to the potty is sacred, it just is. And here's the best part. I would start to walk out and close the door a little to give her privacy and she'd say, "Honey, when you're 95 it really doesn't matter anymore." So I'd kind of squat down on one knee and we would talk about little things while she finished up. Margie and I had a few other potty moments, laughing and talking about whatever happened to be going through her mind at the time.

My potty trips with Margie took me back to when my kids were little and I would talk to them while they were on the potty. It's interesting how being with the dying triggers different memories about life. What a reminder of how much we revert back to being a child when we are dying. It is *so* innocent and lovely. I never forget these moments.

The last time I visited Margie she was lying in bed, just as she did every day, but this time she didn't have the energy to exert herself much at all. That particular day her daughter and son had to be away so it was a special visit, and I was there much earlier than usual. She seemed a little agitated when I walked in, but it was early and I think she just needed quiet and time to wake up on her own. When she started to wake up, she saw me reading and asked me if I needed a light. I told her I was fine, got up and moved closer to her, sitting on her walker like I always did. I told her that I had brought my Bible with chapters marked that spoke of peace and comfort. She was pleased, so we turned off the TV and I started to read to her. Then out of the blue she asked me *the* question I've been asked so many times, "Why am I still here?"

I wasn't sure if I had the wisdom to answer this question, but I contemplated for a moment and then simply shared my experience with this grace-filled Christian woman. "You know Margie," I said. "I think that our soul has a definite plan and it just can't leave until it is complete." She nodded and said that made sense. I also expressed to her that I bet she felt as if she wasn't doing anything or contributing in any way, lying there day after day, to which she also agreed. I continued, "In God's world there is a higher purpose even when we can't see it. That's faith and your soul is finishing up business. When it's done you can go." She agreed with all this and said she was ready whenever God was.

That same day, I happened to glance in Margie's closet where her oxygen machine was kept (these machines are big, noisy and throw off lots of heat). "Wow!" I said, "Look at all those clothes!"

She smiled, "Isn't that terrible?" she said.

"No not at all, I love clothes too. The right outfit for every occasion is fun."

I began pulling dresses out of the closet and we looked them over along with her shoes, and she decided she did not want to be buried in her favorite dress because she felt her daughter would love to wear it. We discussed what she was to be buried in that day.

"That's thoughtful." I said, and Margie told me she thought she would be giving the rest to the church.

"There are many nice things in your closet, Margie," I told her. "Lucky church!" All my conversations with Margie were so beautiful yet matter of fact.

I am not sure when Margie passed away as I had to tend to a family matter at that time. She was amazing and knowing her made me feel like I do think I want to live until I am 90 something. I will always be grateful to Margie for helping me to trust the words that come from my heart.

Chapter 12

Dying Alone

The Survivor receives all people,
even those who don't know what to say,
even those who always seem to say the wrong thing,
even those who don't know what to do,
even those who always seem to do the wrong thing.
Eventually help will come,
and probably in a form I do not except.
—Douglas Corey Smith

In my years working as a hospice volunteer I have occasionally witnessed a separation between patients and their families, which has resulted in dying "alone," without a loved one present. It can be a very sad experience to watch. I have a preacher friend who one day said to me that he didn't know which was harder, dying alone because you have no family, or dying alone because your family stays away, and I had to agree that I didn't know either. There are two women who stand out in my mind as examples of both situations.

IDA

The first day I walked into Ida's room all I could see was a slight woman barely visible beneath the weight of her covers. Her bed was close to the floor and there was a pad next to it and no guardrail was up. I can't imagine this woman falling out of her bed. She was painfully quiet, no words, no expressions, and no movement. Her roommate was screaming and yelling, arms flailing, desperately calling for help. How can a compassionate heart ignore that? The whole scene was just terrible. I went over to the other woman and tried to calm her down for Ida's sake, and then I went out into the hall to grab someone for help so I could be with my patient.

When all had calmed down, I sat on the bed and held Ida's hand. There was barely a hint of who she once was; she was so frail, with no reactions, no words, and very little expression. She seemed terribly sad to me, but that might have been just who Ida was, and this was her journey of dying alone. Ida had been a nurse in her lifetime and had never married nor had children. She did have one friend that would drop by occasionally. Her friend was the only person on her paperwork for family members; I had never seen that before. I did not want Ida to die alone, and thought she might, so I tried diligently to work with the staff at the agency to have vigil volunteers on call. Vigil Volunteers are volunteers who are called out

when there is no family. When the patient is close
to dying the volunteers come in shifts until the
patient passes away.

There is a saying among the hospice
community: *people die the way they have lived.* Ida
died alone. For whatever reason, Ida had always
taken care of others as a nurse, but no one had
ever really taken care of her and this is the way
she died, quietly on her own. What I do know with
all my heart is that Ida was not alone. The angels
were there close by taking care of her.

LORRAINE

Lorraine had lived with her daughter for more
than fifteen years. She was tough and strong willed
and wanted nothing to do with volunteers or
hospice except for a few visits from clinical staff.
When her condition worsened after a bout of
sickness, her daughter immediately put Lorraine
in a skilled nursing facility.

Since Lorraine had been so adamant about
volunteers, I decided to visit her myself, rather
than sending someone else. To my dismay the
rooms at the facility were overcrowded with beds,
there were no windows for them to look out, and
Lorraine's wheel chair practically had to be in the
hall for her to have any view of the TV. No wonder
she was depressed, weepy, and just wanted to sit
in her chair all day long.

There are some assisted living facilities that I really don't like. People may be nice, they may do their best, but in some of these places there's a feeling—an atmosphere—that is really dispiriting. Assisted living or nursing home are the last stop for so many people, and it breaks my heart that we cannot find a way to consistently provide a better experience for the dying. I get so melancholy about this, and I know it is just the way it is, but my heart always wants to make it better.

I could feel Lorraine's pain and sadness as soon as I walked into her room. I asked her a few questions, and she told me she did not understand why her daughter would not talk to her, or why she couldn't go home. I didn't understand either. Lorraine's daughter had barely visited, and then, without any explanation, she stopped coming all together. This was too tough to watch, but there was nothing I could do; it was neither my family nor was it my journey. I sat in silence as Lorraine wept. When I put my hand on her shoulder to comfort her, she recoiled. "Don't you feel sorry for me!" She demanded with authority.

My eyes welled with tears. "I don't feel sorry for you," I said. "I have compassion for you because one day I will be old too." In that instant, I knew that this was exactly what Lorraine needed to hear. Lorraine needed to know that someone cared about her. Ida had died alone but not rejected. Lorraine just gave up one day, stopped eating and left. Just like that. Unfinished business is such a tragedy. Lorraine died alone and feeling rejected.

Who knew what had happened in the history of these ladies' lives? It was an interesting dynamic, two women dying, one with no family to speak of, the other with a daughter who had abandoned her. The situations I have witnessed in hospice have sometimes blown my mind. I often used to wonder why there was no one who loved Ida, and why Lorraine's daughter wouldn't visit her. Withholding love at the end of life is something I just do not understand.

When I speak on the subject of "end-of-life education," it never fails that someone raises the topics of unfinished business and lack of forgiveness. I always tell my students the stories of Ida and Lorraine, because they need to know that even though the person who's dying may have done something in their life that you might not agree with, it's important to remember that it's their *stuff,* their learning journey. My advice is to rise above it, work at it, talk to others, friends or a grief counselor, process it, but please try not to let a loved one leave this earth without forgiveness and love. It will help everyone—on this side and the other. You may even heal lifetimes of pain like I did with my dad. I know it made a difference for him. And it certainly made a difference for me.

Chapter 13

The Mary I Barely Knew

Do not stand at my grave and weep,
I am not there; I do not sleep.
I am a thousand winds that blow,
I am the diamond glint on snow,
I am the sunlight ripened grain
I am the gentle autumn rain.
When you wake in the morning hush
I am the swift uplifting rush
Of quiet birds in circling flight.
I am the soft starlight at night.
Do not stand at my grave and cry
I am not there; I did not die.
—Mary Frye

In addition to my assigned patients there were those who came in to my life out of the blue, so-to-speak. They were people who just happened to be in my life that were dying or had lost someone and needed help. The synchronicities that occurred around these people provided powerful confirmation that we are never alone; we are always looked out for. I believe that if you pay attention to the synchronicities in your life, maintain your faith, and keep an open heart you will always be okay right through to the very end.

Whether it is with a hospice patient or someone I run into by accident who has a terminal illness or has lost someone, assisting people is something I never take lightly. It will always be holy to me, always sacred. I feel such deep emotion about every person I have written about here. While writing this book there were times that I was so overcome with my feelings for the people I helped that I was completely at a loss for words to describe the experience, either verbally or through the keyboard. This happens with death and dying. Sometimes there aren't any words that fit.

Sometimes the celestial committee makes appointments for me. When those opportunities show up I'm always amazed because it is completely unplanned, and it is always such an amazing gift for me as well as for the person I end up spending time with!

One such event occurred when I was in Lake Tahoe on vacation at the Rib Festival with my brother, his adult children, their significant others, and another woman whose name was Mary. As we wandered around the festival my brother told me the story of how Mary's beloved husband had died suddenly. They had been best friends as well as husband and wife. It was that kind of a marriage. Mary and her husband were only in their 50's and had been together a long time. They were living and loving life and enjoying each other when he was diagnosed with lung cancer, though he had never smoked, and he died barely two weeks later.

We continued to roam the crowded festival as we talked. The atmosphere was so happy. People were drinking beer, enthusiastically eating, and lively music was playing. I was taking in the lively energy of the crowd and watching people when I spotted Mary sitting on a bench all by herself. As she looked up at me and I walked toward her we were instantly in our own little world. It was clear that the angels were creating a private space just for us amidst the huge throngs of people.

I squatted down so our eyes could meet and touched Mary's arm. Immediately she began to tell me about how after a year she was still sleeping with her husband's shirt. I assured her that it was okay and that a year was not a long time. She expressed how sad she was, but that she thought she was slowly getting better. Mary had experienced all of the stages of grief but was going in and out of depression.

I asked Mary if she wanted to feel him more, and she said she knew he was around but she could not feel him though she wanted to. So I suggested that she consider creating a special holy place in her room—like a small altar on which she could place a few precious mementos, of her husband. I suggested she might also consider adding a candle to her memorial altar. I personally like to use the votives from the market with pictures of saints and angels on them.

She smiled at me as we talked, because I think the things I suggested were things that had not occurred to her. Grief does that sometimes. It can make one's thoughts cloudy. Yet the realization that heaven is not far away is inherent within us, just waiting to be awakened. These were the little nudges and loving support I wanted to give Mary. I knew I couldn't go home with her and that she would be on her own after I left, just like the little green caterpillar I rescued from the spider web. She definitely had some big "puddles" to get through or go around—birthdays, anniversaries, the holidays, and so on. But I had faith that she would find her way. My sense is we are never done with grief, but as we grow and learn it gets a little easier. Someday Mary will be with her husband and best friend, and he is never far from her at all. Mary is holy just like you are holy, and it is so important to remember this and feel it in your heart. Really feel it.

Earlier in this book I mentioned how I like to buy cards for myself. Often when I am browsing a card will just jump out at me, and I will get a nudge to buy that card and give it to myself, from my angels, (I sign them that way too). I have one card that is about ten years old that I have even loaned to friends at times when they needed a little extra faith. There is so much peace in the beautiful message it expresses:

> (Exterior) FAITH means not needing to see where you are going to know you will get there safely.
> (Interior) You're doing a great job at a very hard time in your life. Even though you can't see what lies ahead, please BELIEVE that you are SAFE and trust everything will work out.

The precious time I spent with Mary was about helping her find peace within her grief by giving her ideas that she could work with to open up her heart and feel safe. I helped untangle Mary from that little spot where she was stuck. Safety was not far away at all. She just needed to know she could get there. Mary looked at me after our conversation and smiled a thank you. I told her she could email anytime, though strangers I help almost never do. But I do know that they always receive whatever help they need from me, because the angels arrange it all.

Think back to a time when you have felt really sad or hurt. How did your chest feel? Did you know they give heart patients a Teddy Bear to hold against their chests after surgery? When your heart hurts physically, emotionally, or spiritually, hugging a pillow close can bring great comfort. On those days when grief is a big dark cloud hovering over your chest, hug a pillow or a teddy bear and just know that deep inside there is a little flame that is flickering. It won't go out. It never goes out. And hope, love, touch, music, nature, candles and yummy smells, will all brighten the light in your heart, ease your burden of grief, and bring you a sense of peace—regardless of the loss you have experienced.

Wherever you may be in your process of grief, if you give love and *be* love, peace will always show its presence, even if it starts with just the tiniest flicker.

Chapter 14

Genevieve

"If you could only sense how important you are to the lives of those you meet; how important you can be to the people you may never even dream of. There is something of yourself that you leave at every meeting with another person."
—Fred Rogers of Mr. Rogers Neighborhood

Genevieve and I started our relationship with one of those casual "hello how are you?" conversations that one often has in passing at the local coffee shop. This continued for about a year, until one day as I was sitting eating my breakfast and reading the paper, this beautiful sparkling singing teacher passed by me with tears in her eyes. I asked Genevieve how she was doing because she looked upset, which was very unusual for her. She started telling me about her dog that had suddenly starting peeing in the house and was making quite a mess of things. She seemed to find this so overwhelming that I immediately knew there had to be something more that was causing her distress. I nodded and listened as she poured out her frustrations and told me of the many difficulties she seemed to be experiencing in her life. Then she said, "Do you know a good massage therapist?"

I smiled at her and said, "You're looking at the best one in town!" I then asked her what the problem was and, with a very sad look on her face, she pointed to her hands and her neck. I reached out to touch her, and in that very instant God touched me. Instantly, the realization flashed through my mind that Genevieve was going to die soon. We set up our first appointment right away.

When Genevieve arrived I walked out to greet her, and as I watched her climb out of her car I knew there was something terribly wrong with her body. She was so unstable on her feet, I couldn't imagine how she was able to stand, let alone walk. I brought her into the house, helped her remove her shirt, and gingerly assisted her onto the massage table. Genevieve warned me it was hard for her to lie on her back, but if she spent a few moments practicing diaphragmatic breathing she would be okay. That statement concerned me, and when I asked her to explain she said she simply was not able to take a deep breath when lying on her back. She truly felt that massage would help her get stronger, and I believe it did, in many ways, but the primary way it helped her was to prepare for what lay ahead. I intuitively knew Genevieve's weakness was from something serious that she was not ready to discuss, so I did the best I could with massage, knowing that gentle loving touch was all I could do for her.

On our second visit she talked about having carpal tunnel surgery and how she felt the surgery would give her back the strength in her hands that she needed. I asked her if she was talking to her doctor about the other weaknesses in her body, shoulders, legs, and pretty much everywhere else. At this point she looked at me, and like a child said, "You know I have the cancer Nina," and like a child I nodded back. It was a precious moment, as if we were children confiding in one another, with a conviction that if we kept the secret we held it would make everything go away.

Genevieve did have carpal tunnel surgery. I was very surprised that she had gone through with the surgery but I felt that this was somehow part of her journey to get ready. A tough one to accept! It broke my heart because right after that she had to go back into the hospital to have even more surgery to relieve some of the symptoms of the cancer and give her a little more time.

When I walked into her hospital room, Genevieve was sitting up in bed, talking with one of her treasured students. They all were treasures to her and she loved them dearly. Her face lit up when she saw me, which was not what I was expecting at all! She looked right at me and said, "You knew, Nina." She meant that she realized I knew all along that she had cancer. I just smiled back and gave her a warm hug and a kiss on the forehead. Genevieve declined quite rapidly after my visit and departed for *Home* a couple of days later, surrounded by her students.

Being with the dying is *so* holy, and I think of Genevieve every time I go into the coffee shop where we met. It is important to know that we are loved beyond measure and to never forget this. Genevieve's story restored my faith that I am always taken care of through challenging times. Genevieve had a son, but she was not married and lived alone. Even so, everything she needed was provided for her journey home. God places people in our life to help us. I believe I helped Genevieve and she helped me. When I look back on my own life and all that I have been through I see that I have always been blessed in so many ways that got me through the tough times. We are all connected and so dearly loved.

Chapter 15

Brenda's Halo

Who knows how long I've loved you
You know I love you still
Will I wait a lonely lifetime
If you want me to, I will.

For if I ever saw you
I didn't catch your name
But it never really mattered
I will always feel the same.

Love you forever and forever
Love you with all my heart
Love you whenever we're together
Love you when we're apart.

And when at last I find you
Your song will fill the air
Sing it loud so I can hear you
Make it easy to be near you
For the things you do endear you to me
Oh, you know, I will
I will.
-The Beatles
(My cousin and her best friend, Brenda's, favorite song)

Brenda was my cousin's best friend. They'd known each other since they were 13 years old. I didn't meet Brenda myself until she was nearly at the end of her life.

I received a call from my cousin Linda, out of the blue, asking me to help her best friend who, at just 46, had been diagnosed as having a very rare form of cancer that had originated in her appendix. According Linda, Brenda's cancer was very deadly, and no one had yet survived it past the five-year mark.

Linda and I are close but we don't speak to each other very often. She began to share with me about what happened to Brenda, at one point, had seemed to be miraculously healed, only to now find out that she was dying. She explained that Brenda had started chemotherapy as soon as she'd been diagnosed with cancer, and after about six months or so, she had confided to Linda that she had been praying a lot and seeing her dad in her dreams. Then, as Brenda has been praying one night something magical had happened; suddenly she felt as though there was a bright light and a burning sensation in her stomach area, and she just *knew* that "something" had happened.

At her next check up, Brenda's doctor had told her that for some unexplained reason her tests were showing a miraculous improvement. In fact, at that point they could not even find the tumor! Upon hearing that news Brenda decided that her miracle gave her the opportunity to do something she had always wanted to do which was to go to Europe. She wanted very much to have this experience with my cousin, and since she knew that Linda couldn't afford the trip, Brenda was going to pay her way.

Off they had gone, best friends celebrating a miracle, playing together, and enjoying each other's company on an incredible ten-day tour of Europe. Soon after they returned from their trip, Brenda's cancer returned full force. In spite of the bad news, Brenda was grateful for the experience, and said she felt that her miracle had been God granting her the chance to travel and spend time with her best friend before she died.

Brenda started another round of chemotherapy but it didn't seem to be helping at all and the doctors didn't give her much, if any, hope. When she couldn't bear it any longer she finally stopped the chemo. By that time her body was so fragile a "halo," which is a metal contraption that fits around the head and is screwed into the skull, had to be placed around her neck and head to keep her neck from snapping and causing paralysis, or worse. Brenda hated the halo and insisted that her son, Ryan, promise that if she had to die with the halo in place, they would remove it immediately upon her death.

The drive to Brenda's for that first meeting was a long one but I didn't mind, as I really wanted to help. Linda told me that Brenda was alone at home most of the time, and she was hoping that I might be able to give Brenda some Reiki, and bring her some comfort and peace.

When I arrived I walked into a very dark house that smelled strongly of cigarettes. As my eyes began to focus I saw that Brenda was lying in her bed in the family room of the house, looking very uncomfortable with her head encased in the halo that was keeping her neck from breaking. Next to the bed was an ashtray stacked with cigarette butts that she apologized for. I reassured her there was no need for an apology.

Brenda told me her son was in his room with the cat watching TV, so I went back to say hello to him before returning to the family room to focus my attention on Brenda.

Brenda was sad, tearful and frustrated with everything; worried about not knowing what was ahead, and feeling scared. The halo was so cumbersome that she could not move her frail pain-wracked body, which made things even worse for her. I sat down beside her and held her hand as I told her that I did massage therapy and Reiki, and was there to do what I could to make her feel a little better. Since it was hard for Brenda to move, I massaged her arms and shoulders, and then gave her Reiki, which relaxed her quite a bit.

I also engaged her in talking about happier times. I wanted to know all about her best friend, my cousin—how they had met, what their favorite things to do together were, and the infamous trip to Europe. We sat talking about these things and I kept her company for a while longer. Before I left I gave Brenda a hug, and as much reassurance as I could about her coming transition.

About a month later my cousin called and asked if I could go to the hospice where Brenda now lived. Of course I said yes. There were five women in Brenda's room when I arrived. One was sitting near the bed but the rest were huddled together, whispering, on the far side of the room It's not uncommon for people to feel confused and uncomfortable around the dying, and I could tell these women weren't sure what to do with their friend who was dying right in front of them.

I walked right up to Brenda, gently placed my hand on her heart, and began sending her lots of love. I stroked her hair and gently whispered to her that she was going to be okay. I was happy to see that the halo had been removed so Brenda could be a little more comfortable during her last days. The lady that was sitting closest to Brenda was a newly trained practitioner who had never used Reiki with the dying before, so I explained how Reiki helped and told her it was wonderful that she was doing this for Brenda.

The other women had drawn closer around the bed but still seemed a little afraid. I spoke up and gently said, "She can hear everything you say, as hearing is the last to go. Please come close to her, stand close to the bed and touch her. This will be so comforting to her." Even though some of them may still have felt uncomfortable, what I shared with them did help on some level.

In the end Brenda left this world as an angel without a halo, for which I was very grateful. I am not sure if the women fully grasped what I shared with them or not, but I do know that something important happened. I was more than happy to have been present to help Brenda pass surrounded by caring friends. She helped me to remember that many do not die with their family around them, and that it is so important to help the living understand the importance—and the necessity— of being fully present, and creating a peaceful and loving environment around a loved one who is actively dying.

Chapter 16

Saying Goodbye to Mom

Warrior

Even when she goes,
*   She's not gone*

Her hands, willing soldiers
Held us all
*   in Safety*
Now tired
*   lay down*

Memory crests
Foaming at the top
A different day
*   turns us over*

Leaves to Soil
Clouds to Sky
When better metaphors
*   Come dancing in*
Inviting me to their everything
table

Upon eating these delicious
meaty morsels

I will know it was her in my
ear, on my tongue,
    there, here, everywhere.

Firefly moments light this
dark night in flashes

Even now
She is asking me
    Telling me

Yelling up the stairs at me
Feeding me
Needing me
Inspiring me
Tiring me
Inspiring me
    to find out who I really am

Interested to know me
before I became this
Red riddle

Pearly grinner,
    my muse and maker
Solid-gold master
    without exception

Her heart
My refuge to realize

Without love
There is no place to dwell
Forever
—Cera Impala, my niece.

Time was growing short for my mom, and it was clear that she had less than three months to live. It took all my faith to get me through the emotions I experienced every day as I watched my mom change before my eyes. There were moments when I had no words to describe my feelings. I was terrified, because I knew my mom was departing this Earth. Her time was running out, and I didn't think I was ready.

During the last couple of weeks of my mom's life I kept an internal journal that will forever be etched in my heart. I want to share my experience with my mother in the hope that if you find yourself taking care of a loved one in transition you'll know you are not alone with the intense feelings that seem to take over when we must let go of someone we love who is dying.

Every time I saw her I felt a sense of urgency to be with her as much as I could. Her decline was evident to me, because I *know* and *feel* things, which can be both a blessing and a curse. My heart wanted to say, "How much longer do I have God? Have I done everything I can do, said everything I need to say?"

I looked at Mom and I wanted to ask her, "Are you okay? Do you want to talk about this journey you're on? Are you afraid of dying? Can I help you with this?"

She had fought this for so long and had done an amazing job, and I wanted her to know she wouldn't be letting me down if it was time and she wanted to go. My heart screamed with the pain I was feeling about losing her, yet the sound never made it to my throat. I had to remind myself that this was her journey, not mine, and she had her path to follow, just like my other patients did.

My day to spend time with Mom was Wednesday, and it had been *our* day for a long time. One Wednesday evening I fed her a scrumptious soup I had made the night before. After she ate she said she was very tired and she was going to go to sleep. Just before she fell asleep, I heard from her room, "I loved the soup. That was so sweet. I love you."

In the past I'd only cooked for my mother a few times, two Mother's Day brunches and three meals at her house. It made cooking this meal all the more special. While she rested I did the dishes and emptied the trash. There was hair piled in the trashcan and I felt a lump in my throat as I fought back tears. I kept telling myself, *It's just the chemo, Nina. It is what happens. You know this.*

I knew she was not going to get better and that she really wanted more time. Of course Mom's journey had always been about fighting the clock. She was always a 'doer' with the desire to get the most out of life. I knew she would continue to take every morsel of living she could get.

As Mom moved along towards her transition we spent many days together, Often I would I would pick dinner up from her favorite noodle house, and then we'd settle in to watch funny movies, Jeopardy, or her favorite crime shows.

We enjoyed a great Christmas Eve dinner together, and Mom shared some hilarious things that night. She really hung in there and seemed to enjoy herself tremendously. The day after Christmas Mom moved in with my sister, and we were all relieved that she had someone with her all the time.

The last three days before Mom passed kind of melted together. The day before my last Wednesday visit with Mom was a big day for her, as it was the first day anyone mentioned the word "hospice" to her. Mom had a wonderful oncologist, who assessed Mom's condition and then gently gave her the news, "The cancer has gotten ahead of us and hospice might be able to offer you more at this point."

My sister, who was with Mom at the time, could see from her reaction that hospice was a word she absolutely did not want to hear. Very upset, she pleaded with her doctor for something more, saying, "I want to live. Isn't there another drug we can try?"

The doctor mentioned there was another chemotherapy she could try, but the drug would not be available until Friday. Mom agreed to try the treatment even though there was virtually no chance that it would help by that point.

My Mom never ever gave up on her life and was clearly determined to live every second, wanting to stay for her kids. I had hoped she was somehow coming to terms with the fact that she was dying, but I felt it was more likely that she was bargaining with God for a little more time, which, knowing my mom the way I did, seemed more likely.

That day only got rougher for her. She had to have more fluid removed from her stomach, which seemed to drain her energy even further, causing a rough night with labored breathing, in spite of the fluid removal.

When my sister reported all of this to my brother and me, we knew in our hearts there was nothing more to be done. The time for chemo was over; the time for saying goodbye was coming.

The following day turned out to be my last Wednesday with Mom. My son Jason rode with me to my sister's house and it rained all the way. It was just rain but it felt like the sky was crying right along with my heart.

When we arrived and I touched my mom for the first time since Christmas Eve, it was a dying person's face I caressed, not the face of my vibrant and lively mother. It was clear that she was no longer fully present. She was tracking, which is when the dying person gazes beyond you or seems to be *somewhere else*. This is part of the soul's preparation for the transition. If I kissed her she would come back to our *dimension* for a few moments, but then she'd drift out again.

I kissed her and kissed her and kissed her.

She seemed so exhausted, and my sister told me she would probably be resting all day, since the day before had been so hard for her. As she left us to visit with Mom, she said, "Keep her comfortable, give her water, and get a frozen Boost down her if you can."

As Jason and I sat with my mom that day I was floored by the weakness in her body. It was hard to believe that just five days before she had been sitting up, eating a meal, and laughing with us on Christmas Eve. She was such a trooper, and her strength of spirit was humbling. But Jason and I knew there was no bouncing back.

Mom's CNA, Grace, got up to take her to the bathroom and I offered to help. Nothing could have prepared me for what I was about to see, even though I'm a hospice worker with 13 years of experience in helping people die.

I was stricken with how frail her body was. It looked like she was 90-years-old. Though I have helped so many dying women to the bathroom, doing this with Mom was so hard. I had to look away for a second, and my throat constricted as I struggled to hold back my tears. I wondered who this woman I was holding up *was*. It couldn't be *my* mom. I loved her so much, and it was terrible to see her like this.

I found myself carrying on a dialogue in my heart. *God, I asked you please, when we got to this point, to do this quick. I've been asking you for weeks. Listen to me please. This is my beautiful, amazing, extraordinary mother! She brought me life, love, and tenderness, and she is suffering! I can't take this God.*

I asked all the angels to surround my mother, hold her, and watch over her.

I believe what they say about how the end it is harder on the survivors than the person who is dying. My heart was in agony. I wanted it to be over for her, but I knew there was no hurrying her process. It is inherent within us to help, and there comes a point that the helping is in the letting go.

At that moment the lessons of letting go were cutting at me like knives. I wanted so much for her struggle to be over, but I recognized that this was part of her journey, and the *in-between* time of her soul's transition was at hand. Mom's soul was completing its journey, finishing its work. Mine was growing and learning. That thought brought love, understanding and peace to my heart.

When we finally got her back to her big comfy chair, I left the room, cried hard, and then I came back.

And I kissed her and kissed her and kissed her.

At dinnertime we tried feeding Mom a little turkey soup my brother, Peter, had brought for her. Mom wanted to be at the table, but she just couldn't hold her head up—she couldn't stay awake. But we tried, Peter and I, to make each spoonful of soup the perfect size to get it into her. She managed to say very slowly, "I want to eat all of it."

I smiled at that statement. It was a metaphor for her life. Mom, food and love have always been synonymous. She never wanted to miss a thing, not even a morsel of my brother's incredible soup.

I kissed her and kissed her and kissed her.

On our way home that night Jason and I had a long talk about his Grandma Noni. I was grateful for his company and he was grateful to have had some time with his Noni.

When I finally went to bed that night sleep wouldn't come even though I was exhausted. My chest felt like there was an elephant sitting on it.

Peter called me at 11:15 am the next morning and told me, "She is not getting up, Nina. Hospice will be here soon for admitting." I felt relieved that hospice was coming.

As I got ready to leave something happened inside me. I felt so tired and weepy. I didn't want to get in the car. The day before had been so tough.

What then began inside my heart was a struggle between what I was *supposed* to do, which meant go and sit with my family and my dying mother, and what I *needed* to do, which was honor my own need to remain separate.

My family was not one of my hospice families. They were my family, and each one of them was preparing for my mother's death in his or her own way. My way is the way of prayer, meditation, Reiki and peace, but not everyone in my family was comfortable with this. My fear was I felt I had some obligation to be at her bedside, like everyone else, when I really felt this wasn't the right thing for me.

Most people don't experience what I do as they watch someone transition. It is scary for them. It was scary for me to watch Mom, too, yet my spiritual understanding allowed me to feel the most incredible love, trust and solid faith. When a loved one dies most people tend to think of their own mortality, which is appropriate and makes sense. Dying is another part of living. Sometimes the loss of a loved one teaches us good things, causes us to make lifestyle changes or maybe even slow down a bit and appreciate the life we have even more. Death offers us an opportunity to do some internal inquiry and soul searching about our life and our inevitable death, *now* instead of waiting until it is actually upon us.

Dying is a sacred event. I just can't say this enough. I wish the whole world could experience the sanctity of it in the way I have. And even though the experience with my mom was different than my experience with my hospice patients and families, the process was still very spiritually powerful.

In those last hours or minutes with a loved one we may wonder about how it feels to die, may marvel at the mysteriousness of the shift from life to death, from breathing to not breathing. We may wonder if our loved one is okay and feel sad about not being able to help him or her cross over. Wouldn't it be great if we were able to escort them to the gate wave good bye and know they were okay? I believe that many of us would like to be able to do that.

In the end, all of my own self-inquiry brought me to the decision not to make the 90-minute trip to Pasadena to be at Mom's bedside with those who were in such a different spiritual and emotional space than I was. My siblings wanted to be there, but I felt like I didn't need to be with her physical body. I wanted to be with her by tapping into our sacred connection from a safe and familiar place. I wanted to be present for Mom alone, and I wanted to help her cross in my own way, through prayer, meditation and tapping into another dimension where I knew I could help—a space that might be uncomfortable or confusing to my other family members.

I was actually surprised at myself for not going to my sister's, but I knew I would regret it all my life if I did not follow my heart. It was my way to remember Mom as she always was, not as the

person in a frail body preparing for the departure
of her soul. There are hospice people to do that. I
chose to hold a sacred loving space for her as she
transitioned, and I am so fortunate to have had the
wisdom to recognize, this time, that being
physically present was not right for me. Being
spiritually present for that sacred moment when
my mother would leave this Earth was the right
choice for me. It was the best decision I ever made.

Mom died peacefully on December 31st. At
the time I was with a dear friend and his family. I
had cooked Mom's delicious fresh marinara sauce
for them, after which we looked at pictures of her
that I had brought with me. We drank some wine
and celebrated her life. I stayed connected to Mom
spiritually the entire time, and later that night the
most amazing thing happened.

It was between 9:30 and 10 pm, and I was
sitting on the couch at my friend's house, when I
suddenly felt Mom. I said to him, "Something's up
with Mom."

I felt squirmy inside, almost like I wanted to
get out of my own body, and then I experienced a
feeling of anxiety in my heart. I walked around for
a minute and then sat back down, closed my eyes
and opened my heart as wide as I could, and said,
"Mom take what you need from my heart. Mom,
it's okay to go, I am right here."

Suddenly I had the most beautiful crystal
clear vision of a bright white rope coming out of

my heart. I saw her hand holding onto the rope, and that's when I said, "It's okay to let go." It was so vivid that I knew it was real.

My brother called minutes later and confirmed what I already knew—Mom was gone.

I knew at that moment I had made the right decision not to be physically present with her. She needed me in spirit.

At times, the grief process has been very sad and overwhelming for me. Even though I understand she is in a better place and I have accepted her death, there are days when I feel as if a tidal wave has hit me. The tears come and refuse to stop. The first year of firsts without her was been incredibly hard—first Mother's Day, first Christmas, Easter and birthday. Each event provided another time of grief and a new opportunity to let go, a little at a time, through a deluge of tears. Even after the passage of time I still miss her. I still want to pick up the phone and call her for a friendly chat. I also smile and my heart expands when I feel her in a gentle breeze, in the rustle of leaves up in the trees, and in the rush of water as it ebbs and flows when I sit near the ocean. She is with me every single day.

I am with my mom even though she isn't on the physical plane anymore. I love her so much, and I know we are together always in our hearts.

* * *

When Mom finally left this earth I was okay,
because I had let her know what an incredible
mom she was and how she did a great job raising
me. We moms always hope we did a good job,
because we did the best we could. Hearing it is
important.

Thank you God for the many gifts you have
bestowed upon me, for my tongue and my voice so
that I could share my story with others, and for my
hands and heart that I might offer love and healing
to those who need it. My heart swells with
gratitude for all the amazing gifts of my faith.

I wish for you, the reader, many blessings in
this life. Enjoy living. Play. Laugh a lot. Love deeply
and learn to let go. And know that when it's time
for you to go, your departure will be a holy
celebration of this life as you cross over, with love,
into the next one.

Acknowledgments

I would like to express my love and gratitude for the following people:

Tonie Impala for your words that will forever stay in my heart to remember to always follow mine as it will never steer me wrong.

Joseph Impala for teaching me the invaluable lesson of compassion for myself and others

Maria Impala, Peter Impala, Joseph Impala Jr. for being there and making the effort to understand me even though I know it has not always been easy, and for helping me remember the details of our childhood.

Cera Impala. Your beautiful poetry speaks to my heart and needs to be shared, thank you,

My gifts, Andrew and Jason Murphy, for believing in their mom and the path she has chosen. How fortunate I am to have your love and support in my life.

Pauline Ward-Townsend for stepping in
and giving me a mom's loving words on
those hardest days.

Pam Stevenson who was always just a
phone call away and will be forever in my
heart.

Pamela Coyne who has weathered many
storms with me and has given me
tremendous support with insight and love
for her dearest friend.

Jesse Ramos for never letting me forget
how important it was to keep going with
this little book no matter what happened,
reminding me of what it meant to complete
it.

Carol Holaday, my editor, who knew what
to do with my excitement and passion
when my stories seemed to pour out of me
faster than I could write.

Sandie Sedgebeer for being my cheerleader
and believing in me on so many levels, and
understanding the importance of this
subject and the need to make it known.

Last but not least, to all the souls that have gone before me who helped me to write this book. Your stories live on here and will help many. Thank you for being a part of my life and thank you for all the blessings you constantly bestow on this humble human being. You have gifted me with so much.

About the Author

Nina Impala is a professional educator in the End-of-Life Field. Certified by The American Academy of Bereavement for Spiritual Facilitation for the Terminally Ill, **Nina** also holds a bachelors degree in Human Services and is a graduate of Mueller College.

For well over decade **Nina** has worked passionately as a hospice volunteer, visiting the dying and educating families and other volunteers. In addition to actively working with one or two hospice patients at any given time, **Nina** offers individual counseling, facilitates grief groups and speaks from her *Tutoring for the Spirit*/*HeartSight™* series at a variety of venues in the Southern California area. Her desire is to help people of all ages feel at peace with themselves and with the transition process. She is also a Reiki Master and massage therapist.

Nina lives in Temecula, California near her two sons. She enjoys bringing education to her community about the transition from this life, a subject that has been sorely neglected in our society.

For more information visit her website at www.tutoringforthespirit.com

Made in the USA
Las Vegas, NV
20 September 2024